THE BELOVED DISCIPLE

Tom Jacobson

BROADWAY PLAY PUBLISHING INC
New York
www.broadwayplaypublishing.com
info@broadwayplaypublishing.com

First printing February 2014
I S B N: 978-0-88145-573-1

Book design: Marie Donovan
Page make-up: Adobe Indesign
Typeface: Palatino
Printed and bound in the U S A

PUBLISHED BY B P P I

BUNBURY

THE CHINESE MASSACRE (ANNOTATED)

EAT THE RUNT *(written as Avery Crozier)*

THE FRIENDLY HOUR

HOUSE OF THE RISING SON

TAINTED BLOOD

OUROBOROS

THE TWENTIETH-CENTURY WAY

ABOUT THE AUTHOR

Tom Jacobson has had more than 70 productions of his plays in Los Angeles and around the country, including SPERM at Circle X Theatre Company, THE ORANGE GROVE at Playwrights' Arena, and the award-winning BUNBURY, TAINTED BLOOD and OUROBOROS at The Road Theatre Company. He has been a co-literary manager of The Theatre @ Boston Court, a founding member of Playwrights Ink, and a board member of Cornerstone Theater Company. He teaches playwriting and related courses for U C L A Extension. His most recent productions were THE FRIENDLY HOUR at The Road (*L A Weekly* Award for Best Ensemble), THE TWENTIETH-CENTURY WAY at The Theatre @ Boston Court and the New York International Fringe Festival (five Ovation Award nominations, four Los Angeles Drama Critics' Circle nominations, one GLAAD Award nomination, Fringe Festival Award for Outstanding Production of a Play), and MAKING PARADISE: THE WEST HOLLYWOOD MUSICAL for Cornerstone (Critic's Choice in *Back Stage West*). The world premier of THE CHINESE MASSACRE (ANNOTATED) was recently at Circle X, and THE HOUSE OF THE RISING SON was cited by *The Los Angeles Times* as the Best New Play of 2011 after its world premiere at Ensemble Studio Theater—L A.

THE BELOVED DISCIPLE premiered on 7 July 1994 at The Complex in Los Angeles (Tom Jacobson and Andrew Campbell, Producers). The cast and creative contributors were:

CHRISTOPHER MARLOWE .... Cully Fredericksen
EARL OF SOUTHAMPTON .... Matthew Wagner
ACTOR .... Robert Kerbeck

Director .... Fred Sanders
Set & lighting design .... Al Schnupp
Costume design .... Christina Wright

CHARACTERS

ACTOR, 29, *nondescript, with a high or balding forehead, thoughtful and introverted until he bursts into life playing other roles that include:*
THOMAS KYD, 35, *a repressed playwright*
JUDAS ISCARIOT, 29, *a persuasive manager with a hump*
CONSTABLE DINGLEBERRY, 45, *a simpleton with authority*
QUEEN ELIZABETH, 60, *imperious and brilliant*

KIT MARLOWE, 29, *a charismatic playwright plagued with cynicism and a hot temper; also plays:*
JESUS CHRIST, 33, *a gentle revolutionary*

HENRY WRIOTHESLEY (HARRY), 19, *the rich and beautiful Earl of Southampton; also plays:*
JOHN, 19, *a disciple of* JESUS

SETTING

The action takes place in London and environs in May of 1593. The play within the play is set in Judea in approximately A D 30.

Because the stage must at times be a torture chamber, the hall of an upper-class English home, the shore of Galilee, a tomb, the upper room of an English inn, the upper room of a home in Jerusalem, and Queen Elizabeth's antechamber, the setting must be simple and versatile, with scene shifts created primarily through lighting. In ACT ONE, three chairs and a table are required. In ACT TWO, a bed replaces the table. In both ACTS two entrances and a window are required.

Costume note: Period costumes are neither required nor discouraged.

ACT ONE

(Darkness. A crashing drumbeat or percussive sound effect as an isolated light reveals the ACTOR *[as* THOMAS KYD*] tied to a chair next to a table. He wears a moustache, brown wig and poor, almost rustic, attire. He looks very nervous.)*

ACTOR: *(As* TOM*)* Let the clouds scowl, make the moon dark, the stars extinct, the winds blow, the bells toll, the owl shriek, the toads croak, the minutes jar, and the clock strike twelve: I will not speak!

(Blackout. Percussion. Lights up, revealing the ACTOR *still seated, but with his head turned to one side and blood dripping from his mouth.)*

ACTOR: *(As* TOM*)* I'll speak. My name is Thomas Kyd, but 'tis not my work. I know not whence it came.

(Blackout. Percussion. Lights up, revealing the ACTOR *with his hand resting on the table, each of his fingers in a diabolical metal device. He looks at them with more curiosity than fear.)*

ACTOR: *(As* TOM*)* Papist pilliwinks, you say? A more afflicting pinch than English thumbscrews?

(Blackout. Percussion. Lights up, revealing the ACTOR *with an pained expression on his face and blood oozing from the pilliwinks. After a moment he relaxes enough to regard the pilliwinks with admiration.)*

ACTOR: *(As* TOM*)* An admirable tweaking. I must find a place for it in my next comedy.

(Blackout. Percussion. Lights up, revealing the ACTOR *in the same position, but with more blood on his face. His look of pain has intensified to agony.)*

ACTOR: *(As* TOM*)* Tragedy, then! No insult was intended. *(Reacts as if to a threatened blow)* I've said all I can. Those scribbles are not mine.

(Blackout. Percussion. Lights up, revealing the ACTOR *with his head thrown back and blood running from one ear.)*

ACTOR: *(As* TOM*)* I am no atheist!

(Blackout. Percussion. Lights up, revealing the ACTOR*, his head hanging forward. Slowly he raises his face; his nose is bleeding.)*

ACTOR: *(As* TOM. *Slowly, with venom.)* Cursed be the demon that mingled his scurrilous blasphemies with my honest draughts. He shared my writing cell nigh on two years ago, but I have shunned his tainted company since. *(Reacts to a threatened blow)* His name? *(Chuckles)* His name.

(Blackout. Percussion. Lights up, revealing the ACTOR *twisted violently to the right.)*

ACTOR: *(As* TOM*)* Marlowe!

(Blackout. Percussion. Lights up, revealing the ACTOR *twisted violently to the left.)*

ACTOR: *(As* TOM*)* Marlowe!!

(Blackout. Percussion. Lights up, revealing the ACTOR, *still seated, lying face-down across the table sans pilliwinks. He looks up.)*

ACTOR: *(As* TOM*)* My beloved Kit.

(Blackout. Percussion. Very different lighting slowly comes up, revealing the ACTOR *in the same position but without the moustache and wig and staring at his bloody hand. Facing him and seated in a chair some distance away is* HARRY, *the nineteen-year old* HENRY WRIOTHESLEY, *Earl*

of Southampton. He is a beautiful, delicately feminine youth with remarkably long flowing hair and gorgeous aristocratic clothes.)

ACTOR: Let the clouds scowl, make the moon dark, the stars extinct, the winds blowing, the bells tolling, the owl shrieking, the toads croaking, the minutes jarring, and the clock striking twelve. And then at last, sir, starting, behold a man hanging, and tottering and tottering, as you know the wind will wave a man, and I with a trice to cut him down. And looking upon him by the advantage of my torch, find it to be my son Horatio!

HARRY: *(He applauds the* ACTOR*'s performance.)* Brilliant interpretation!

ACTOR: But 'tis not over.

HARRY: I know the rest. I've seen *The Spanish Tragedy* twice.

ACTOR: Thou'lt see it no more. The playwright's been arrested.

HARRY: Thomas Kyd?

ACTOR: And tortured, so I hear.

HARRY: Why?

(Suddenly there is an insistent knocking on the door. The ACTOR *looks at* HARRY *questioningly;* HARRY *responds with an almost impatient, but graceful gesture toward the door. The* ACTOR *starts toward the door.)*

HARRY: The blood!

*(*HARRY *throws the* ACTOR *a cloth. The* ACTOR *sheepishly tries to wipe the blood from his face as he walks, stoop-shouldered, to the door. He opens the door, revealing* KIT MARLOWE, *a handsome, bearded man of 29. He wears clothes barely a cut above the* ACTOR*'s. They stare at each other in shock.)*

KIT: My God—an actor! *(Heartily embracing him)* Reduced to service, my good...Winnie?

HARRY: *(Shakily pointing a small knife at* KIT*)* Hold, sirrah! Touch him not.

(As KIT *steps away from the* ACTOR*)*

HARRY: Who are you...sir? And from whither? I hope you may pardon my unwelcome greeting, but I am not uncautious of the plague. My wenches have all died—

KIT: Hast employed this bloody bubunkle in their stead? A traveling player, promiscuous leper of the stage, a posse commitatus of disease convoked to wreak mortality upon an enfeebled house?

HARRY: Is that true?

ACTOR: I'm an actor. We get around.

HARRY: How'd you know?

KIT: I'm a poet. We're worse. But staunch thy windows with the herb of grace and rue, throw cold water before thy door in the evening—and the infection may spare the master of the house.

HARRY: And prayer.

KIT: Prayer. Pray forgive me my interruption of thy intimate scene—such private plays play best when both audients are actors. This hallowed hall is no place for poets.

HARRY: *(As* KIT *turns to leave)* You're really a poet?

KIT: Knowst me not? The saint who bore our Saviour Child across the whelming flood, and bore as well the weighty sins of all the world—including thine?

HARRY: Christopher...Marlowe? *(Delighted, lowering the knife)* You sent me that filthy story—

KIT: Filthy *poem*!

HARRY: *(Attempting to quote)* When both are liberated, love is slighted—is that right?

ACTOR: Where both deliberate, the love is slight:

Who ever lov'd, that lov'd not at first sight?

KIT: My verse has passed so quickly into common parlance?

HARRY: I desired his opinion.

KIT: What do actors know of verse, but how to cripple it?

ACTOR: I liked it.

KIT: You did? *(To* HARRY, *pulling manuscript pages from a satchel)* But I've brought thee better.

HARRY: A play?

KIT: As yet a playling, a mere masque—but with thy fair assistance—

HARRY: *(Flattered)* Assistance?!

ACTOR: Generosity.

KIT: *(Annoyed)* Thy help—

ACTOR: Thy patronage.

KIT: *(Losing his temper, to the* ACTOR*)* And why are you here—character study?! *(To* HARRY, *impassioned)* Since March of ninety-two the plague's closed the theatres, starved the players, pummelled playwrights into poverty. *(Kneeling)* An humble dramatist, I kneel before thee—like pampered jades of Asia bowed beneath the lash of Tamburlane—

ACTOR: —'sblood! He's quoting himself.

HARRY: Oh. You want money.

*(*KIT *looks at the floor.)*

HARRY: Save thy passions for the groundlings. 'Tis true, I am disposed to patronize the stage, to render

help, assistance, gold, as I am pleased. But the Lord
Treasurer Burghley—whose ward I am for yet another
year—hath curtailed my revenue of late. *(To* KIT*)* As
much as I admire thy verse— *(To the* ACTOR*)* —And
thy grotesque and bloody deeds upon the stage—to
poets, players, and the like I'm forced to be ungenerous
these days.

(Sheepish, KIT *stands.)*

HARRY: —I can support but one.

*(*KIT *and the* ACTOR *fall to their knees.)*

ACTOR: I have not words—

KIT: I do.

ACTOR: And can only touch thee with feeling.

KIT: With but a pained expression on thy face?

ACTOR: And with the cries of my poor unfed babes.

KIT: Yes, don't omit the starving brats. *(To* HARRY*)*
They'll eat thy very heart with sorrow. *(To the* ACTOR*)*
Though you can make him weep—

ACTOR: And crow for joy, shriek with terror, shake
with anger, pine for love, rage with hatred—

KIT: *(Holds up the manuscript)* I offer immortality.

HARRY: I'm…in there?

KIT: Who knows what paltry players mimed
Agamemnon, Orestes, dying Iphigenia? But heartless
Clytemnestra and her brood live on, their very breath
the poet's words.

(A gurgling sound interrupts. KIT *and* HARRY *both stare at
the* ACTOR*.)*

KIT: Was that your stomach?

ACTOR: No.

HARRY: Do you truly starve?

ACTOR: 'Tis nothing.

HARRY: *(Getting his purse)* My heart is conquered—by thy belly. If thy brats are hungrier still—my regrets, poet.

(As HARRY *starts to hand the* ACTOR *the purse,* KIT *intercepts.)*

KIT: I understand. Feed his belly now to feed your soul. But I cannot stomach poetry defeated by a gurgle. Let him prove his talent worthy of thy love—and use my words to earn his daily bread.

ACTOR: No.

HARRY: I've chosen—

KIT: Three weeks! For three weeks only subsidize us both. Keep us here to honor thee with tales and passions—let him act my pages as the ink falls from my pen, and in conclusion make thyself the victor's patron.

HARRY: Honor me with tales…?

KIT: And passions.

HARRY: *(To the* ACTOR*)* What say thee?

ACTOR: Three weeks—of food?

KIT: And drink, and beds.

HARRY: Of course.

KIT: *(Handing out manuscript pages to both)* It's such a part, Gil, as you've never seen!

ACTOR: My name's not Gil.

HARRY: I'm to act as well?

KIT: As will I. Shall we play a scene and then choose whether to proceed?

HARRY: I'm no actor.

KIT: *(Energetically tearing down a white drape)* When Burghley said you were to marry his granddaughter, were you in any wise ecstatic?

HARRY: I gave an answer and a smile that pleased him well.

KIT: Acting! *(Almost an aside to the* ACTOR*)* Anyone can do it.

HARRY: *The Beloved Disciple*? 'Tis a mystery play?

KIT: *(Draping himself)* 'Tis tragedy! A subject most sublime.

ACTOR: The passion of Our Lord?

KIT: Oh, no—the story of a poet!

HARRY: Who?

KIT: You! Saint John—the author of the Gospel. Your costume…

ACTOR: And who am I? What's the role?

KIT: Judas Iscariot. We're casting by type.

ACTOR: Are there many lines?

KIT: *(Picks up a shift, shows it to* HARRY*)* Thy saintly robe.

HARRY: That's my wench's gown!

KIT: *(Pulling the gown over* HARRY*'s head)* 'Tis only for a play, where boys ape women; thou shalt ape a saint—

ACTOR: —The furthest thing from woman.

KIT: *(Wadding up cloth, to the* ACTOR*)* You'll need a bunchback as well.

ACTOR: Judas had no hump.

KIT: *(Sticking the wad up the back of the* ACTOR*'s shirt)* Were you there? 'Tis symbolic of thy deformed soul.

ACTOR: And who are you—in this poet's tragedy?

KIT: The only role remaining. A minor one: Jesus Christ. *(Consults the manuscript)* Act one, scene one: the shore of Galilee.

(As KIT *becomes* JESUS, HARRY *becomes* JOHN *and the* ACTOR *becomes* JUDAS, *they change drastically.* JESUS *is physically and vocally quieter than* KIT; *he doesn't move much or very quickly, but exudes calm authority.* JOHN *is much more masculine and energetic than* HARRY; *he speaks loudly and passionately, and moves without* HARRY's *accustomed grace. As* JUDAS, *the* ACTOR *gains strength; even with his hump he has dignity. The acting is somewhat declamatory [particularly* HARRY's*] but grows more naturalistic as the play within the play progresses. As this scene progresses, the actors wean themselves away from the manuscript pages.)*

KIT: *(Reading stage directions)* Enter Jesus and John, wet.

*(*KIT *douses himself and* HARRY *with water from a pitcher.)*

KIT: *(As* JESUS*)*
It gives me wonder great as my content
To see you here before me. O my soul's joy!
If after every tempest come such calms,
May the winds blow till they have waken'd death!
My soul hath her content so absolute
That not another comfort like to this
Succeeds in unknown fate.

HARRY: *(As* JOHN*)* The heavens forbid
But that our loves and comforts should increase
Even as our days do grow!

(They embrace somewhat awkwardly as the ACTOR *douses himself with water and makes his entrance.)*

ACTOR: *(As* JUDAS. *Aside)* Oh, well tun'd now!
But I'll set down the pegs that make this music,
As honest as I am.

(JESUS *and* JOHN *find towels and dry each other and themselves.* JUDAS *dries himself.*)

HARRY: *(As* JOHN*)*
The sky it seem'd would pour down stinking pitch
But that the sea, mounting to th' welkin's cheek,
Dash'd the fire out. Poor souls, they would
Have drown'd but for thy word that calmed the sea
And thy sure footsteps treading on the wave.

(JESUS *hands* JOHN *a pen and parchment, urging him to write.*)

HARRY: *(As* JOHN. *Writing)*
"A ghost! A spirit-demon!" Thomas cried.
And Andrew cowered in the washed bow
Amid the froth and spittle of the sea
Until thy clearest words touch'd all our souls:

KIT: *(As* JESUS*)* Be of good cheer; 'tis I; be not afraid

ACTOR: *(As* JUDAS*)*
Then Peter, solid ass, call'd "Lord, if it
Be thou, then bid me come to thee upon
The flood!"
(To JESUS, *exasperated)*
And straightaway thou bidst him walk!

KIT: *(As* JESUS. *Calmly, with a shrug)*
Hast tried to stay our Peter from his wont?
'Twas more to gain by giving him his due.

ACTOR: *(As* JUDAS*)*
To watch our Peter sinking as a rock
And foundering in foamy, swirling wrack?
Disciples are too hard to win to lose
By drowning them like kittens in a sack!

KIT: *(As* JESUS*)*
I caught his fainting hand and pull'd him to
My side with words design'd to cool his fever'd
And perturbed brain—

HARRY: (*As* JOHN. *Writing*)
—Perturbed brain—

KIT: (*As* JESUS) Pray do not record my every word.

(JOHN *writes this down.*)

KIT: (*As* JESUS) "Oh, thou of little faith," I whispered in
His ear, "Wherefore didst thou doubt?"

ACTOR: (*As* JUDAS. *Laying a small carpet at* JESUS' *feet.*)
But did he not perceive the raft on which
You stood, afloat and tow'd behind our craft?

(JESUS *steps onto the carpet and pulls* JOHN *to him to
demonstrate.*)

KIT: (*As* JESUS. *Slightly annoyed with* JUDAS.*)*
He clutched me thus in terror lest he fall
Into the raging Galilean lake,
His eyes directed skyward, unto God.
"Look not upon the water," I did warn,
"But turn thy faithless gaze upon the Lord."

ACTOR: (*As* JUDAS)
(*Laughing and pulling the carpet like a raft*)
Thus question'd, faith must prove itself more strong!

KIT: (*As* JESUS)
And had he seen the barge he'd yet believe.

HARRY: (*As* JOHN. *Stepping away from* JESUS, *disturbed*)
This miracle was crafted in thy brains
And not an holy benefice or boon?
A strategem, a ruse, a patent fraud?

ACTOR: (*As* JUDAS) Be not so fond as to imagine all
Thou seest is true.

KIT: (*As* JESUS) How faith is found is not
Among our Father's great consuming cares.
(*Indicating the parchment*)
But write of its discovery on the lake.
Thou mayst omit the part about the raft.

HARRY: (*As* JOHN)
But water into wine, and loaves and fish
That feed five thousand souls—!

ACTOR: (*As* JUDAS) Much gold and not
A little silver spent to sate that mob's
Unruly and voracious appetite.

KIT: (*As* JESUS)
Didst thou believe my words of peace and love
Afore these supernatural events?

HARRY: (*As* JOHN. *Reluctantly*) No.

KIT: (*As* JESUS)
And now that thou hast stopp'd to hear me speak
And listen'd once thou sawst the pretty signs,
Dost disbelieve the music of the phrase
Because the flute that play'd it's a machine?

HARRY: (*As* JOHN) No.

KIT: (*As* JESUS)
What have we stolen with sweet tricks but what
Is freely giv'n? For love alone is our
Required fee, and open ears and hearts
To learn of love.

ACTOR: (*As* JUDAS) A little lucre would
Preserve our famished souls from death e'en so.

KIT: (*As* JESUS)
'Tis written man lives not by bread alone
But by the words proceeding from God's mouth

ACTOR: (*As* JUDAS) Full bellies open ears.

KIT: (*As* JESUS) Their gullets we
Have gently stuffed with miracles and bread.
A new commandment I give unto you
Love ye one another e'en as I
Have loved you. By this shall all men know
That ye are my disciples if ye love.

But for that love, day would turn to night!
A wither'd hermit, fivescore winters worn,
Might shake off fifty, looking in love's eye:
O, 'tis the sun that maketh all things shine!
Come, kiss me with the kisses of thy mouth
Thy love is sweeter still than honey wine—

ACTOR: *(As himself)* Stay! Cease thy wicked words!

(The ACTOR *tears off the hump, and* KIT *and* HARRY *relax and begin to take off their costumes.)*

KIT: 'Tis a first draught.

ACTOR: A draught of blasphemy!

KIT: *(Relishing the accusation)* Dearest Phil, 'tis only a play.

ACTOR: A deadly toy, a bewitching bauble! And my name's not Phil!

HARRY: The words are comely and the verse has grace—

ACTOR: But such words in Our Lord's mouth!

KIT: 'Tis only meet and proper that our Saviour speak of love.

ACTOR: 'Tis hardly Biblical! More nearly…carnal!

KIT: The Word made flesh. I confess Christ sings the Song of Solomon, therefore 'tis most Biblical. *(Peers out the window)*

ACTOR: Thou hast plagiarized and abused thy source, the Holy Writ.

HARRY: These speeches of love to me seemed…most seemly. And not unlike the courtly speeches…at court.

KIT: Aye. 'Tis for an educated audience the play is writ.

HARRY: *(Excited)* Don thy armor, poet. Actor, mount thy attack! The battle's on—thou art engaged! Let's read some more.

KIT: Not yet. *(Leaning out the window, hollering)* How much for those medlars, sweet? *(Turning the* HARRY*)* Aren't you hungry? *(To the* ACTOR*)* We know you are. *(To* HARRY*)* Can you send your acting-servant out for apples?

HARRY: *(Pulling out his purse, while the* ACTOR *glares at* KIT.*)* 'Tis truly a starving profession—my own belly growls after only these scant verses!

(In awkwardly handling his purse, HARRY *dumps its entire contents—many coins—out on the table.* KIT *and the* ACTOR *refrain from leaping to get their hands on the money, but if any coins fall to the floor, they pick them up and pocket them.)*

HARRY: How much are apples?

ACTOR: Tuppence.

HARRY: Pence? I have none. Take thee a crown.

(The ACTOR *takes the coin and dashes out the door.* HARRY *plays casually with the coins as* KIT *sits beside him, uncomfortably close. They smile at each other,* KIT *confidently,* HARRY *nervously.)*

HARRY: What draws thee to Our Saviour…as a subject?

KIT: 'Tis a logical progression in my tragedies. Tamburlaine the Great—an infidel who defied Mahomet. The Jew of Malta, by his very nature accursed of God. Edward the Second—

HARRY: That one I saw.

KIT: Didst thou? And? Did it charm thee?

HARRY: Charm? Edward struck me over-fond of Gaveston, and the manner of his death—

KIT: A red-hot poker in the fundament? 'Tis the actual history of proud England.

HARRY: How leadest these to Christ?

KIT: Each flouted—as you say—or challenged God. Our blessed Saviour claimed the appellation for Himself.

HARRY: Claimed?

KIT: *(Moving even closer)* Proclaimed. And after all their miserable deaths—by poker, fiery fever and boiling oil—

(The ACTOR *comes in with some sad little apples.)*

KIT: —I desired a hero who could not die.

ACTOR: *(Putting the apples on the table)* Your hero shall never live—on any London stage. The Master of the Revels must censor it and censure you.

HARRY: Was there no change?

ACTOR: None, sir.

*(*HARRY *looks suspicious as the* ACTOR *tries to look innocent.)*

KIT: My play shall fare as well as any in London this plague-season.

ACTOR: True—there are no plays in shut-up theatres. The scourge has killed more actors—

KIT: And poets.

ACTOR: Lord Pembroke's company's gone bankrupt—

KIT: They owe me yet for *Faustus.*

ACTOR: *(Thumping the manuscript)* These blasphemies will only earn you years in Hades. Jesus Christ as Machiavel—or worse!

(They start eating the apples. KIT *bites into his with juicy abandon, and has soon devoured several. The* ACTOR, *though starving, tries to be polite and eat slowly.* HARRY *rather prissily finds his knife and cuts his apple into slices.)*

HARRY: We've only read scene one. Certainly a play may not be judged until the bows, for what comes last illumes what goes before.

KIT: See, fair Billy—

ACTOR: Don't call me that!

KIT: —The blessed innocence and clarity of youth! Condemn not Machiavels. *(To* HARRY*)* You'll need their skills at court.

HARRY: Her Majesty liketh me well.

KIT: Should Narcissus survive his own enamor'd looks to age into a man, 'tis Ulysses' wiles our sovereign then esteems.

HARRY: Hast done her service?

KIT: Her Majesty sent me on holiday to France—then asked to see my travel-journal.

HARRY: A spy?

KIT: Serving princes maketh one princely.

*(*KIT *points to the oblivious, gorging* ACTOR*.)*

KIT: I offer thee those skills. Shall we resume the play?

ACTOR: Not on thy life.

KIT: *(Sighs and winks at* HARRY*)* An author, I suppose, doth out-Machiavel Machiavelli. For like Our Lord, the poet begets worlds, populates, and runs them.

ACTOR: Thy words are mine, to pummel, rape, put to death, and resurrect as I please. Thou art at my mercy.

KIT: Doth thy wife and bairns know thou rapeth language for their bread?

ACTOR: *(Rapidly scanning through the manuscript pages)* Give me but a line. Ah. *(Puts down the manuscript and delivers the line straight)* By being seldom seen, thou couldst not stir

But like a comet thou art wond'red at,
That men would tell their children "This is he."
(By inserting his own punctuation, he mangles the sense.)
By being seldom seen? Thou couldst *not* stir!
But—like a—comet? Thou art wond'red at that men.
Would tell their children "This is he?"

KIT: *(Feigning annoyance, while* HARRY *laughs.)* He's
come so far since Zenocrate.

HARRY: Zenocrate?

KIT: The principal female in *Tamburlaine,* the king's
wife. He possessed a less scanty pate in those days.

ACTOR: She was an insipid drab till I got hold of her.

KIT: You made her a queen.

ACTOR: And can crown myself king—or like the
halting beggar limp, or steely soldier march. Hang my
natal star o'er any realm— *(In a French accent)* —Zee
state of France— *(In a German accent)* —Clock-builting
Chermany— *(In an Italian accent)* —Machiavelli's owna
Italy. *(His own voice)* Or turn my timbre and my stance
to any of the seven ages, from— *(Acts like a silly child)*
—Prattling youth— *(Acts senile)* —To prattling, palsied
eld. *(Eyes* HARRY *and* KIT.*)* You've no defense 'gainst
mummers' jibes. *(Imitates* HARRY'*s voice and gestures)*
Her Majesty liketh me well.

(When KIT *laughs, the* ACTOR *imitates him.)*

ACTOR: Serving princes maketh one princely. *(His
own voice.)* The more parts I play, the more worlds I
conquer.

(The ACTOR *stares at them triumphantly.* KIT *glares back.)*

KIT: But he never could memorize lines.

(The ACTOR *glares at* KIT *for a moment, then pops the hump
back on and snatches some of the coins and begins counting
them as* JUDAS*—without consulting the manuscript.)*

HARRY: (*Worried about his money*) Hey!

ACTOR: (*As* JUDAS)
Prophet thou art, and Messiah, and shalt be
What thou art promis'd. Thou wouldst be great,
Art not without ambition, but without
The boldness should attend it.

KIT: (*Handing* HARRY *the manuscript and taking one
himself.*) 'Tis the play! But he's skipped to his big scene.
(*Aside to* HARRY, *winking*) He memorizes in a wink—
and no actor can resist his cue.

(HARRY *and* KIT *don their costumes to become* JESUS *and*
JOHN.)

ACTOR: (*As* JUDAS. *Overlapping*)

Hie thee hither,
That I may pour my spirits in thine ear,
And chastise with the valor of my tongue
All that impedes thee from the golden round,
Which fate and metaphysical aid doth seem
To have thee crown'd withal.

(*Seeing* JESUS *and* JOHN *approach,* JUDAS *tries to hide the
coins.*)

KIT: (*As* JESUS) Iscariot,
Whence gold? Or rather, whither go'st?

ACTOR: (*As* JUDAS) The poor,
Who lack in all but lack itself, must needs
Be sated with more nourishment than words.

(JESUS *nods to* JOHN *who confiscates the coins from* JUDAS.
Both JUDAS *and the* ACTOR *are disappointed. Both* JOHN
and HARRY *are relieved.*)

KIT: (*As* JESUS. *Smiles knowingly*)
But what advancement may we hope from them
That hath no revenue but their good spirits
To feed and clothe them? Why should the poor be

flatter'd?
They'll be with us for aye, and we with them.

ACTOR: (As JUDAS. *With distaste)*
But yet not in among them, for their stain
May be avoided and their burning wounds
Be salv'd by coinage dropped from outstretched hand.
'Tis time to keep a distance from the mob.
Could such inordinate and low desires,
Such poor, such bare, such lewd, such mean attempts
Accompany the greatness of thy blood,
And hold their level with thy princely heart?

KIT: (As JESUS. *Amused)*
What princely? And what greatness? I have ne'er
Been more than conduit of words that from
Our Father flow, but not of noble blood
Of any wise. A carpenter I am.

ACTOR: (As JUDAS)
If thou so lavish of thy presence keep
So common-hackney'd in the eyes of men,
Opinion, that could help thee to the crown,
Will still keep loyal to possession,
And leave you in reputeless banishment,
A fellow of no mark or likelihood.
By being seldom seen, thou couldst not stir
But like a comet thou art wond'red at,
That men would tell their children "This is he."

KIT: (As JESUS)
Or like the rare-seen ostrich, "What is that?"

(JOHN *and* KIT *laugh.)*

KIT: (As JESUS)
Judas, friend, forget these crowned kings,
For how can mighty monarchs speak of love?
Would such a sovereign say that thou
Must love thy enemies, do good to them
That hate you? Bless him who curses you—

(JOHN *writes furiously.*)

KIT: (*As* JESUS. *Gently, but pointedly directed at* JUDAS)
And pray for them who spitefully use you.
And unto him who smiteth thy one cheek,
Turn to him the other smiling thus.

(JESUS *smiles and departs.* JUDAS *watches* JOHN *write.*)

ACTOR: (*As* JUDAS)
Thy copied platitudes will feed no babes,
Nor break for us the hated yoke of Rome.

HARRY: (*As* JOHN. *Continuing to write*)
Thy thoughts swim in the shallows of the sea
Of testing time. Jerusalem and Rome
Shall flooded by forever be, and sink
Beneath the wave of all eternity.
(*Indicating his parchment*)
But thoughts writ here like islands in the main
Will harbors prove for future hearts of men.
(*Reading*)
And unto him who smiteth thy right cheek,
Turn unto him thy left, and he who takes
Thy cloke away, forbid him also not
To take thy coat. To every man that ask,
Unto him give, and from him who thy goods
Doth take ask not for them again. As ye
Would have men do to you, do unto them.

ACTOR: (*As* JUDAS)
How now? That's not the speech I heard him make.

HARRY: (*As* JOHN)
He would have said—he went on in that vein.
Posterity will understand for I
Have much more clearly rounded out the sense.

ACTOR: (*As* JUDAS)
How else hast thou improv'd upon his speech?

HARRY: (*As* JOHN) But not a whit.

ACTOR: (*As* JUDAS) A little?

HARRY: (*As* JOHN) No.

ACTOR: (*As* JUDAS) A jot? A tittle?

HARRY: (*As* JOHN) Only when his statements may
Offend.

ACTOR: (*As* JUDAS) For instance?

HARRY: (*As* JOHN) When he speaks of love.

ACTOR: (*As* JUDAS)
He does so without cease! Dost alter all?

HARRY: (*As* JOHN)
I script him vague when he'd specific be.

ACTOR: (*As* JUDAS) Aye, I like not that.

HARRY: (*As* JOHN) What dost thou say?

ACTOR: (*As* JUDAS)
Nothing, my friend; or if—I know not what.

HARRY: (*As* JOHN)
Dost like not how our lord doth speak of love?

ACTOR: (*As* JUDAS)
This love he vaunts, 'tis equal to each sex?

HARRY: (*As* JOHN)
As pure and chaste to each. Why dost thou ask?

ACTOR: (*As* JUDAS) But for a satisfaction of my thought,
No further harm.

HARRY: (*As* JOHN) Why of thy thought, dear Judas?

ACTOR: (*As* JUDAS)
Doth love he them as he hath loved you?

HARRY: (*As* JOHN)
'Tis what he preaches and he lives his word.

ACTOR: (*As* JUDAS) Indeed!

HARRY: (*As* JOHN)
Indeed? aye, indeed. Discernst thou aught in that?
Is he not honest?

ACTOR: (*As* JUDAS) Honest, my friend?

HARRY: (*As* JOHN) Honest? Aye, honest.

ACTOR: (*As* JUDAS) Dear John, for aught I know.

HARRY: (*As* JOHN) What dost thou think?

ACTOR: (*As* JUDAS) Think, my friend?

HARRY: (*As* JOHN)
Think, my friend? By heaven, thou echost me,
As if there were some monster in thy thought
Too hideous to be shown. Thou dost mean something.
I heard thee say even now, thou lik'st not that,
Of love too specified. What didst not like?
And when I said he loved all as myself
With constant and ne'er-changing heart, thou criedst
  "Indeed!"
And didst contract and purse thy brow together,
As if thou then hadst shut up in thy brain
Some horrible conceit. If thou dost love me
Show me thy thought.

ACTOR: (*As* JUDAS) For our friend Jesus,
I dare be sworn I think that he is honest.

HARRY: (*As* JOHN) I think so too.

ACTOR: (*As* JUDAS) My friend, I see y'are mov'd.

HARRY: (*As* JOHN) No, not much mov'd;
I do not think but Jesus is most honest.

ACTOR: (*As* JUDAS)
Long live he so! and long live you to think so!
(*As himself, breaking character, taking off the hump*)
Enough! I cannot utter more!

HARRY: (*As himself*)
Methinks there is much here that is unsaid.

ACTOR: *(To* KIT*)* What dost thou imply?

HARRY: This love is noble friendship, courtly admiration. Our Saviour and the beloved disciple shared a bond most—

ACTOR: Greek.

HARRY: Yes, like Spartan warriors, pledged to one another. A manly love transcending the lustful embraces of the female sex.

ACTOR: Then why does Judas play upon it so, with such success? And thy secondary theme, of tampered phrase, augmented parables—the words came not from God?

KIT: Every poet's inspiration comes from God—if one is a theist.

HARRY: Dost disbelieve?

KIT: Consider only that the Indians and many authors of antiquity have assuredly written of above sixteen thousand years ago, whereas Adam is proved to have lived within six thousand years.

ACTOR: You could burn for such rhetoric!

HARRY: Take care, our actor friend doth memorize thy speeches word for word.

KIT: We've inherited a faith of fishermen and base fellows of neither wit nor worth. Paul only had wit, but he was a timorous fellow in bidding men to be subject to magistrates against his conscience. 'Tis late. Hast thou a bed for me?

ACTOR: *(When* HARRY *looks at him)* I'll not fluff pillows for an heretic.

KIT: Then I must off. Pity. I'd hoped to find a quiet place to write.

HARRY: *(Leaping up)* Nay, tarry! I'll make thy bed myself!

(Glancing at the ACTOR *with annoyance,* HARRY *goes out.* KIT *quickly turns to the* ACTOR.*)*

KIT: Dost like the play?

ACTOR: You'd be a better playwright if you'd work on your acting.

KIT: The writing, sirrah!

ACTOR: Many a speech is surpassing fair. But Jews as heroes? 'Tis not commercial.

KIT: Dost move thee like *The Passionate Shepherd to His Love?*

ACTOR: 'Twas a poem—and for a different purpose writ.

KIT: *(Touches the* ACTOR*'s shoulder)* But for the same—to obtain a patron's love.

ACTOR: *(Regards* KIT *a moment, smiles sadly, and turns away)* Then 'tis the patron that hath changed. What thinkst thou of our lordship?

KIT: I much admire his youth—the cleanness of his thought. An innocence that's most beguiling.

ACTOR: *Tabula rasa?* Art anxious to scribble on his slate?

KIT: Those who love not tobacco and boys are fools. His hair doth ravish.

ACTOR: 'Tis a comely lad, but none too bright.

KIT: His genius lieth not within his skull, but upon it.

ACTOR: Gulled by the stomach trick. *(Makes his stomach gurgle)*

KIT: 'Twas charity I let you get away with that old mummer's device.

ACTOR: Do you yet admire my mumming?

KIT: Thy bony wife, thy famished brats? The haste with which you gobble apples?

ACTOR: 'Tis no act. My wife and babes do starve.

KIT: I'm sorry.

ACTOR: I meant within your play, as Judas.

KIT: 'Twas not a poor performance, but as an actor, like Sampson, thou hadst more power with hair. *(Pulling out some coins, offering them)* Buy thy babes some bread.

ACTOR: Thou hast as great a need.

KIT: Not so dire.

ACTOR: Then why are you here? I'll not beg from a beggar.

KIT: Let it be my widow's mite.

ACTOR: Walsingham's abandoned thee.

(KIT is silent a moment, then sighs and pockets the coins.)

ACTOR: Why else would you go begging patrons door to door?

(As the ACTOR turns away, KIT slips the coins in the ACTOR's pocket.)

ACTOR: Thy temper fouled thy nest again, dear Kit. A loss of dignity. The soaring eagle mocking like a crow, till all within earshot want to wring thy neck.

KIT: Walsingham called me "over-enthusiastic". Am I?

ACTOR: Thou art "over" everything! Canst not be quiet, nor calm, nor listen for a while? 'Twould profit thee among thy peers and lend subtlety to thy dialogue as well.

KIT: Dost insult mine ear?

ACTOR: Th'advice is gratis—'tis all thou canst afford.

KIT: While thee thy faces pull, and mew and fart and whine upon the stage—my words shall charm our lord above the stench of thy putrid playing!

ACTOR: Thy poesy won't be heard above the gross guffaws my droll antics draw forth, or shall founder in the tearful ocean my pathos pleads!

KIT: Thy false emotions!

ACTOR: Thy leaden words!

KIT: Thou—actor!

ACTOR: Thou poet!

(HARRY appears.)

HARRY: How now?

ACTOR & KIT: *(Quickly turning to him, bowing slightly)* My lord.

HARRY: Shall rash conduct decide the race?

KIT: We fought over thee, my lord. Thy profile doth seem princely to mine eye—

ACTOR: —Compelling me to argue for an angel's countenance—

HARRY: My profile is flattered—

(KIT and the ACTOR smile.)

HARRY: —But my purse is flattered more. Thy beds are ready.

(HARRY gestures and they follow.)

HARRY: A most fawned-upon chambermaid, I.

(KIT follows HARRY out, with the ACTOR close behind. Before the ACTOR disappears, he takes out the coins KIT slipped him, and bites one; he's known they were there all along. As soon as they are gone, the lights change to isolate a chair and a corner of the table. KIT sits down and begins to write. On the other side of the stage, HARRY

appears with manuscript pages. While KIT *writes,* HARRY *reads; they both do so with great intensity. After a moment of concentrated writing and reading,* KIT *smiles with satisfaction and* HARRY *follows suit almost immediately in reaction to what he has read. Throughout this writing/ reading sequence,* HARRY'S *movements echo, amplify, or somehow relate to those of* KIT; *it is a duet, and as sensual as possible.)*

*(*KIT *chuckles;* HARRY *giggles.* KIT *writes, leaning forward;* HARRY *leans backward to read.* KIT *laughs;* HARRY *gasps.)*

KIT: Ah.

HARRY: *(Softly)* No!

*(*KIT *blows gently on the ink to dry it;* HARRY *blows his long hair out of his eyes.* KIT *writes rapidly;* HARRY *traces the words with his fingers at the same pace.* KIT *mumbles as he writes;* HARRY *mouths the words.)*

KIT: *(Scratching out a line)* Fie.

HARRY: Hmm?

*(*KIT *drags his fingers roughly through his hair;* HARRY *fluffs his locks luxuriously.* KIT *starts writing on a new parchment;* HARRY *begins to read a new page.* KIT *touches the pen to his tongue;* HARRY *licks his lips.* KIT *absently scratches his thigh as he writes;* HARRY *rubs his.* KIT *belches;* HARRY *coughs nervously.* KIT *writes faster, slightly opening his shirt;* HARRY *strokes his own chest.* KIT *sniffs;* HARRY *sighs.)*

KIT: Aha.

HARRY: Ohhh.

*(*KIT *scratches his crotch;* HARRY *lays his hand gently on his crotch.)*

KIT: Uh-huh, uh-huh—!

HARRY: Ahhh!

KIT: Yes!

(KIT *kisses the manuscript; simultaneously* HARRY *kisses his. The* ACTOR *appears near* HARRY *and watches him.*)

HARRY: Yes!

(KIT *continues to write silently, but with great animation.*)

ACTOR: Sweet heresies, my lord?

HARRY: No! Yes—sweet, yes. But methinks not heretical.

ACTOR: Would thy guardian agree?

HARRY: Burghley is an ass—and a dried-up one at that. I've given these new pages close scrutiny, and found myself, not them, wanting.

(*The* ACTOR *just stares at* HARRY.)

HARRY: Wanting—more! More verses!

ACTOR: I have more verses for thee.

HARRY: (*Reaching for the parchment the* ACTOR *proffers*) Act Three?

ACTOR: (*Holding it away from* HARRY) In time, my lord. Hast pondered Lord Burghley's question?

HARRY: He wants another answer so soon? I am too young, unexperienced, as yet unmanly, to merit so fine a maid as Lady Vere.

ACTOR: Hast aged six months since.

HARRY: I'll go to Burghley when I've more to say. What pays he thee to ply me with these queries? (*Grabs the page from the* ACTOR, *looks at it*) 'Tis not the play.

ACTOR: I only said 'twere verses.

HARRY:
A woman's face with Nature's own hand painted
Hast thou, the master-mistress of my passion…
A man in hue, all hues in his controlling,

Which steals men's eyes and women's souls amazeth.
And for a woman wert thou first created;
Till Nature, as she wrought thee, fell a-doting,
And by addition me of thee defeated,
By adding one thing to my purpose nothing.
But since she pricked thee out for women's pleasure,
Mine be thy love, and thy love's use their treasure.

(HARRY *looks at the* ACTOR, *who just smiles at him.*)

HARRY: I don't get it.

ACTOR: *(Exasperated)* Think on it a while.

HARRY: 'Tis very complimentary...of my hues. And
says I should have been a woman—

ACTOR: But yet thou hath that part that women
treasure.

HARRY: My hair?

ACTOR: Treasure—in men.

HARRY: *(Giggles)* The sense, then, is most clear!

ACTOR: That you shall marry Elizabeth Vere.

HARRY: But...why would Kit write thus?

ACTOR: He didn't!

HARRY: Hath a very dirty play on "pricked."

ACTOR: 'Twas mine! 'Tis my sonnet.

(HARRY *looks very puzzled for a moment, then gets angry.*)

HARRY: Thou hast made thy poem a bawd in service of
Lord Burghley!

ACTOR: A sweet persuasion—

HARRY: Now soured by thy falsity. I'm more
persuaded to dismiss thee from my sight—

ACTOR: Nay, my lord—

HARRY: The poet bests the actor when the actor acts not for himself!

ACTOR: —Let me stay.

(HARRY stares at the ACTOR a moment, evaluating his sincerity.)

HARRY: Prove thy love.

ACTOR: How?

HARRY: *(Holding up* KIT'*s manuscript)* Play with me this scene—I want to hone my mumming.

ACTOR: At thy insistence, else I would not.

(The ACTOR *dons the hump, and* HARRY *wriggles into his robe.)*

HARRY: 'Twill please Kit to see me act John well.

ACTOR: Thy natural act will please him in the part.

HARRY: *(As* JOHN. *Still somewhat stiffly)*
In sooth, I know not why I am so sad;
It wearies me, thou sayst it wearies thee—

ACTOR: *(As himself)* Aye, thy playing wearies me.

HARRY: *(As himself)* What?

ACTOR: Must I play all the parts? Thy John's a lump, a dullard—I've seen more expressive logs. *(Imitating* HARRY, *woodenly)* In sooth, I know not why I am so sad. *(Himself)* Because you cannot act.

HARRY: I can too! Kit said—

ACTOR: He's no actor. How can words inspire emotions in the groundlings when they're muttered without feeling? If John is melancholy, thou must find thy tears, tap the melancholy of thy life.

HARRY: I can't just *be sad.*

ACTOR: A history play like this is but a metaphor for the present. Situate the story in today—what grieves

thee now? A loss of favor with the Queen? Thy witheld
fortune?

HARRY: *(Tries to summon emotion, can't)* I cannot.

ACTOR: Then 'tis hopeless.

HARRY: *(Sadly)* I'm sorry.

ACTOR: Let us plod grimly on.

HARRY: *(As JOHN. Sadly, and therefore much improved.)*
In sooth, I know not why I am so sad;
It wearies me, thou sayst it wearies thee,
But how I caught it, found it, or came by it,
What stuff 'tis made of, whereof it is born
I am to learn;
And such a want-wit sadness makes of me,
That I have much ado to know myself.

ACTOR: *(As JUDAS)* Why then thou art in love.

HARRY: *(As JOHN)* Fie, fie!

ACTOR: *(As himself)* Pathetic.

HARRY: *(As himself)* 'Tis not the line.

ACTOR: Thy acting moved me much—to scorn. It lacks
life, fire.

HARRY: Must needs insult—?!

ACTOR: Not insult—instruct.

(ACTOR impatiently waves for HARRY to continue.)

HARRY: *(As JOHN. Angrily, much better)* Fie, fie!

ACTOR: *(As JUDAS)*
Not in love neither? Then let us say thou art sad
Because thou art not merry; and 'twere as easy
For thee to laugh and leap, and say thou art merry
Because thou art not sad. Now by two-headed Janus,
Nature hath fram'd strange fellows in her time,
(Produces a vial)

But even thou in melancholy frame
Wilt laugh at this most curious fond toy.

HARRY: *(As* JOHN*)* 'Tis curious but will it yet cure me?

ACTOR: *(As* JUDAS*)*
Thou art immune, unless thou liest and doth
In truth but pine for love.

HARRY: *(As* JOHN*)* A draught of love?
A Gentile taint begins to stain thy thought.
Such sorceries are sins against our faith.

ACTOR: *(As* JUDAS*)*
'Tis from a Gentile bought—a Greekish witch.
But think not of this liquor as a drug,
Instead a quaint amusement worth a smirk,
And therefore constituting thee a cure.
See, thou hast even now succumbed, as I
Did when I heard the seller's tale of how
This weak solution wreaks a pow'rful end.
Wast so enchanted by the witch's words
I paid a piece of silver for the yarn
And got the potion as a bonus gift.

HARRY: *(As* JOHN*)*
Then salve my sadness with your Greekish lore.

ACTOR: *(As* JUDAS*)*
This beldam Greek did spy upon a time
Flying between the cold moon and the earth,
Cupid all arm'd. A certain aim he took
And loos'd his love-shaft smartly from his bow,
As it should pierce a hundred thousand hearts;
But she did see young Cupid's fiery shaft
Quench'd in the beams of the wat'ry moon,
And mark'd she where the bolt of Cupid fell.
It fell upon a little western flower,
Before milk-white, now purple with love's wound,
And maidens call it love-in-idleness.

Fetched she that flower, and from its dainty juice
Distilled this potent potion here.

HARRY: *(As* JOHN*)* Oh, yes,
And whoso drinks this hearty broth will love
Whoever 'tis that placed it in his hand.

ACTOR: *(As* JUDAS*)*
Not so, said she, for I bethought the same.
'Tis he desirest love that drinks the draught;
Its properties will draw the love to him.

HARRY: *(As* JOHN*)*
A merry jest—hast shown this to our friend?

ACTOR: *(As* JUDAS*)*
The sin of it would shame his silly sense.
I dare not flout this rude joke in his face.

HARRY: *(As* JOHN*)*
Then give it me, and I will jest with him.

ACTOR: *(As* JUDAS*)* But if no fable, then a hazard's here.

HARRY: *(As* JOHN*)*
No hazard in my hand, 'tis but a trick.

ACTOR: *(As* JUDAS*)*
'Tis surely safest spilled upon the ground.

HARRY: *(As* JOHN*)* An empty vial's no good—

ACTOR: *(As* JUDAS*)* For what, dost say?

HARRY: *(As* JOHN*)*
A voided vial will drain the joke of juice.
Dost want thy coin? I'll buy thy tricky drink.

ACTOR: *(As* JUDAS*)* 'Tis evil luck to buy a joke. If thou
Must have the liquor and the legend both,
Then freely will I give.

HARRY: *(As* JOHN. *Proferring coin)* Take this.

ACTOR: *(As* JUDAS*)* Oh, no.

HARRY: *(As* JOHN*)*
If not for thee, then for the suff'ring poor.

ACTOR: *(As* JUDAS. *Simultaneously, taking the coin.)*
—Then for the suff'ring poor.

HARRY: *(As* JOHN*)*
Thanks, Judas. I will yet make Jesus laugh.

(They both laugh as JUDAS *leaves. As* JOHN *seriously contemplates the vial,* JUDAS *reappears, but* JOHN *does not see him.)*

ACTOR: *(As Judas. Aside, tossing the coin)*
Wilt cry before he laughs, for thou hast bought
A dram of poison, such soon-speeding gear
As will disperse itself through all the veins
That the life-weary taker may fall dead,
And that the trunk may be discharg'd of breath
As violently as hasty powder fir'd
Doth hurry from the fatal cannon's womb.
(He leaves.)

HARRY: *(As* JOHN*)*
I have a faint cold fear thrills through my veins,
That almost freezes up the heat of life.
What if this mixture do not work at all?
What if this joke 'tis truly only that?
By faith—he's said, I've writ—a mountain can
Perforce be moved.
(To the vial)
My faith shall stir thee up
And thou shalt stir his love and bend to me
His sole affection. Jesus, canst thou love?
Not every human face, but only mine!
Not poor and bleeding flesh, but comely, young—
But soft! Beware good John, of jealousy!
It is the green-ey'd monster which doth mock
The meat it feeds on. The cuckold lives in bliss
Who, certain of his fate, loves not his wronger;

But O, what damned minutes tells he o'er
Who dotes, yet doubts; suspects, yet strongly loves!
(To the vial)
'Twill amend with thee; I pray that thou be true.
(Drinks)
But how to pray about a pagan draught?
My Hebrew father doth despise such spells—
Wilt Zeus or Venus answer me, a Jew?
Shalt murmur Latin or in Greek entreat?
Perhaps to Cupid, whose disarming bolt
Wounded first the flower of this brew.
(Doubles over in pain)
The pang of love hath wounded me as well!
Could it be venom rather than a drug,
A murd'rous poison, adder-sprung and foul?
My sisters, help! Thy brother's broiled in pain!
Good Mary, Martha, bear me to my bed!
O, false apothecary! Pagan death!

(JOHN dies. The lights on JOHN/HARRY fade. Throughout, across the stage, KIT continues to write. At the moment of JOHN's death, he leans back, exhausted. The ACTOR, as TOM, stumbles into the room wearing the moustache, brown wig and bloody bandages on his fingers. Emotionally as well as physically scarred by the torture, TOM now lives in a permanent state of paranoid anxiety, occasionally twitching, and frequently looking over his shoulder.)

ACTOR: *(As TOM)* Kit.

KIT: Tommy!

(Forgetting, TOM proffers his bandaged hand; KIT shakes it and TOM winces and groans in pain.)

KIT: Brawling again, Tommy?

ACTOR: *(As TOM)* Aye, brawling with— *(Looks about suspiciously)* —Her Majesty's chief torturer. 'Twas no contest.

KIT: Thou never wast a fighter. Why art thou here?

ACTOR: *(As* TOM*)* I have confessed thy name.

KIT: And which of my offenses dost confess? All London knows my follies—I'll tell them myself, unpersuaded by the pilliwinks.

ACTOR: *(As* TOM*)* Our writing room near Saint Paul's was pillaged by the magistrates and all the parchment's confiscate.

KIT: 'Twill be released, 'tis no evidence to be feared— arresting plays!

ACTOR: *(As* TOM*)* Among the pages was an early draught of yours.

KIT: Which?

ACTOR: *(As* TOM*) The Beloved Disciple.* Scanty portions of some Acts, so thy name did not appear.

KIT: Until you named it.

ACTOR: *(As* TOM*)* Aye. I could not act a hero's part.

KIT: 'Tis little matter. Her Majesty knows me.

ACTOR: *(As* TOM*)* Wouldst torture for a little matter? And who informed on me? *(Touches his chest, winces)* Shall I never write again?

KIT: Thou shalt. But act not hastily—for thy fingers' sake.

HARRY: *(Rushing in with manuscript pages and costumes)* Kit, Act Three is fabulous—!

KIT: Harry—Lord Southampton—this is Thomas Kyd.

HARRY: *(Shaking* TOM*'s hand)* The playwright? I loved *The Spanish Tragedy.*

(Seeing TOM*'s wince, then his hand.)*

HARRY: What's happened to thy hand?

ACTOR: *(As* TOM*)* An accident.

KIT: *(Simultaneously)* Fisticuffs.

ACTOR *(As* TOM*)* & KIT: Accidental fisticuffs.

HARRY: *(Gently examining the hand)* Thumbscrews.

(Looks at TOM *for confirmation;* TOM *and* KIT *stare.)*

HARRY: You've been tortured.

KIT: He named my name as propagating libels. But 'tis no fretting thought—

HARRY: For I shall clear thee with the Queen. *(To* TOM*)* Go below stairs—my servant shall tend thy hand.

KIT: 'Tis that actor, Tom, my old Zenocrate.

ACTOR: *(As* TOM*)* What was his name? Weldon? Wimple?

KIT: Whittlesby?

ACTOR: *(As* TOM*)* I saw him only days before—Kit, did he know of thy play—?

KIT: *(Practically pushing him out of the room)* Hurry down and let him heal thy hand.

ACTOR: *(As* TOM*)* He bears us some ill will—!

KIT: Before you hemorrhage on the floor!

(When the ACTOR/TOM *is gone,* KIT *turns to* HARRY.*)*

KIT: Wouldst thou indeed defend me to the Queen?

HARRY: I have her favor, I have told thee.

KIT: Have I thine to such degree?

HARRY: *(Holding up the pages)* As Christ incarnates God, thy words incarnate worth. I love thy play. Hast written more for me?

KIT: *(Holding up pages)* Act Four, scene one. But you need not plead before the queen. My fledgling Machiavel.

HARRY: *(Taking the pages)* Let's play it now.

KIT: And fledgling actor, too. Very well.
(Laying him down on the table.)
Thy part is simple; thou art dead.

HARRY: *(Donning his robe)* I know—'tis daring to slay
the title character by Act Three.

KIT: *(Covering HARRY with a sheet)* Perhaps 'tis not.

HARRY: Not slain? Oh, let me not be slain. You deviate
drastically from your source.

KIT: *(Putting on his drape)* Drama is deviation.

(Becoming JESUS, KIT kneels beside JOHN's body.)

KIT: *(As JESUS)* With fairest flowers
Whilst summer lasts and I live here, dear John,
I'll sweeten thy sad grave.

ACTOR: *(As JUDAS. Stepping into the scene, hump on.)*
Prithee have done,
And do not play in wench-like words with that
Which is so serious. His sisters wail
Without this stony tomb; thou canst afford
No weakness of ambition here within.
Thy miracles have risen in a pitch
That calls for nothing less than death's defeat.

KIT: *(As JESUS)*
Immure me here within. Thou blessed thing,
God knows what man thou mightst have made, but I;
Thou diedst, a most rare boy, of melancholy.

ACTOR: *(As JUDAS)*
Lack not in iron courage at this pass!
The opportunity shan't come again
To prove thy life divine by saving his.

KIT: *(As JESUS)*
I know when one is dead, and when one lives;
He's dead as earth. Lend me a looking-glass,
If that his breath will mist or stain the stone,

Why then he lives. Is this the promised end?
And my poor fool is dead! No, no, no life!
Why should a dog, a horse, a rat, have life,
And thou no breath at all? Thou'lt come no more,
Never, never, never.

ACTOR: *(As* JUDAS*)* Was the hope drunk
Wherein you dress'd yourself? Hath it slept since?
And wakes it now to look so green and pale
At what it did so freely?

KIT: *(As himself)* Hold now!

ACTOR: *(As himself)* What?

KIT: Dost rewrite the play?

HARRY: *(Sitting up)* What's wrong? Why are we
stopping?

(The ACTOR *and* KIT *push* HARRY *down.)*

KIT: He paraphrased my verse.

ACTOR: A minor improvement.

KIT: Improvement?!

ACTOR: You said "sick and pale". I—

KIT: Substituted "green". How dost improve?

ACTOR: The assonance of "green" doth link the phrase
with "freely" in the line thereafter.

HARRY: *(Sitting up)* That's very good.

KIT: *(Pushing* HARRY *down)* I thank thee for thy
contribution. But please refrain from further
emendation.

ACTOR: Twas but to demonstrate an actor has the last—
and oftimes better—word. *(Becomes* JUDAS*)*
Was the hope drunk
Wherein you dress'd yourself? Hath it slept since?
And wakes it now to look so green and pale
At what it did so freely. From this time

Such I account thy love. Art thou afeard
To be the same in thine own act and valor
As thou art in desire? Wouldst thou have that
Which thou esteem'st the ornament of life,
And live a coward in thine own esteem?

KIT: (As JESUS) My friend is dead.

ACTOR: (As JUDAS) And thou canst make him live!

KIT: (As JESUS) Just as I trod upon the sea and fed
Five thousand souls, made wine, with sleight of hand?

ACTOR: (As JUDAS)
The steel hath been heated for the blow.
Thou art the smith with hammer in thy fist
To forge thy fate, then cool it in acclaim.
The mourning crowd without believes you can.

KIT: (As JESUS) Hast told them I shall try?!

ACTOR: (As JUDAS) Shalt do.

KIT: (As JESUS) My fate is forged by these forged feats.

ACTOR: (As JUDAS) Be thou now Messiah or no man.

(JESUS *stares almost malevolently at* JUDAS *for a moment,
then tenderly takes* JOHN's *hand. He sighs, lifts his other
hand, hesitates, then falters. Suddenly, his body stiffens, as
if possessed, and his face and voice take on great authority.*
JUDAS *smirks.*)

KIT: (As JESUS) I am the resurrection and the life,
Whoso believes in me, though he were dead
Yet shall he live. And whosoever lives
And doth believe shall have eternal life.
Believest thou this?

(JOHN *suddenly grips* JESUS's *hand and pulls himself up.*)

HARRY: (As JOHN) With all my heart, my lord.

(JESUS *cries out in shock and joy,* JUDAS *in horror.* JUDAS,
in fact, flees and disappears. After a moment, JESUS *embraces*
JOHN.)

HARRY: (*As* JOHN)
Thou mad'st me live. I heard thy call and came.

KIT: (*As* JESUS)
And thou mad'st me I know not what, a god?

(*Face to face in the embrace,* HARRY *breaks the scene.*)

HARRY: 'Tis a moving scene.

KIT: Thou art moved?

HARRY: I am much enamoured—of thy verse.

(KIT *lets* HARRY *go and takes off the drape.* HARRY *takes off
the robe.*)

KIT: Thou hast inspired it. Christ's eulogy doth mourn
for thee.

HARRY: But I am not dead.

KIT: In some wise dead to me.

HARRY: (*Stares, uncomfortable, then changes the subject*)
The traitor is just as clearly molded in the image of our
actor friend. Wherefore dost thou hate him so?

KIT: I once wrote him some verses he rejected.

HARRY: I'll not reject them. Thou knowst I am
betrothed—

KIT: Yes.

HARRY: —Somewhat against my will.

KIT: Grant not thou thy will its will, it will perforce
have its will with thee.

HARRY: I sense I am too…young to make my way with
women.

KIT: Thou art only wanting in instruction.

HARRY: Teach me, then.

KIT: Laboring in the labyrinth of love, every youth needs an elder Theseus to pass to him that tested ball of twine.

HARRY: *(Giggles)* Else will kiss a minotaur in error?

KIT: Shalt start with that avoidance? Kissing ill?

HARRY: 'Tis most to be afeared.

KIT: Then thou shalt be thy lady—Elizabeth?

HARRY: Elizabeth Vere.

KIT: Commence, then, thus. *(Stroking* HARRY*'s hair)* Fair Lizzie, I do love thy locks.

HARRY: Must I Lizzie be? Why not you?

KIT: Thou shalt imitate my acting of thy part. Fair Lizzie— *(Nods)*

HARRY: *(Stroking* KIT*'s hair)* I do love thy locks.

KIT: *(Stroking* HARRY*'s cheek)* Progress in thy caress from tresses meandering down the cheek, gently grazing the ear, thus.

HARRY: *(As he progresses from* KIT*'s hair to his cheek)* Hast thou a phrase for this procedure?

KIT: Thy lips must form no words, but a smile, which sayeth more. Forget not the ear.

HARRY: *(Going back for the ear, abruptly and roughly)* Oh, sorry!

KIT: Dig not so. Thou art not mining wax. Graze. Like gentle chewing sheep.

HARRY: Graze.

*(*KIT *slowly pulls* HARRY*'s face to his.)*

KIT: Now sly advantage take of thy wanton hand's introduction to thy lover's face and acquaint thy lips with his.

HARRY: Hers.

(KIT *just smiles, closes his eyes and slowly, gently kisses* HARRY's *lips.* HARRY *keeps his eyes wide in terror and anticipation until the moment their lips meet. After this very light kiss,* KIT *lets go of* HARRY's *face and opens his eyes.* HARRY *keeps his eyes closed for a few moments, overwhelmed.)*

KIT: Forget thee not to breathe.

HARRY: *(Pulling* KIT's *face to his)* 'Twill come with practice.

(Another light, brief kiss)

KIT: Thou hast matriculated the school of courtly kissing. Art prepared to study for thy Master's?

HARRY: Yes.

KIT: Soften thy lips, and part them—

*(*HARRY *does so instantly.)*

KIT: —Upon my approach. Part thy fair teeth as well and free thy reckless tongue from its pearly prison. Make not thy tasting tongue too stiff and jab it thus— *(Sticks out his tongue, jabs it about)* —Like a lustful lizard.

HARRY: How shall I do?

KIT: Caress the cavern of my mouth as thy hand meandered though my hair. The journey is the joy, as much the destination.

HARRY: I'll follow thee.

(Gently but with barely restrained passion, they kiss at length. Just as the restraint is beginning to give way, the ACTOR *bursts in upon the scene as* DINGLEBERRY, *a portly, dimwitted constable. As* DINGLEBERRY, *the* ACTOR *wears a padded paunch, spectacles, and a large, drooping hat.)*

ACTOR: (*As* DINGLEBERRY) By God and the Queen's grace, cease and resist!

(*Somewhat stunned,* KIT *and* HARRY *break their embrace.*)

ACTOR: (*As* DINGLEBERRY) Art either thou the playwright Marlowe or Henry Wriothesly, Lord Southampton?

HARRY & KIT: I am.

ACTOR: (*As* DINGLEBERRY) Pray which is which?

KIT: I, Marlowe.

HARRY: And I, Southampton. And pray, who art thou, atrespass in my house?

ACTOR: (*As* DINGLEBERRY) Dingleberry, a constable and the Queen's man.

KIT: The Queen is to be pitied. She has a hanger-on.

ACTOR: (*As* DINGLEBERRY. *Grabbing the script pages from the table*) Ah, the manuscript.

KIT: Thou art a wise constable. And this a table, this a chair.

ACTOR: (*As* DINGLEBERRY) Acting on the Queen's behalf, I am charged to confiscate this unholy play, as it is most reverent.

KIT: Who charged thee?

ACTOR: (*As* DINGLEBERRY) Her Most Dishonored Majesty.

HARRY: And how came she to know of it?

ACTOR: (*As* DINGLEBERRY) I am too wise and worldly, as you say, to diverge such information. (*Looks at the pages*) 'Tis a major work.

HARRY: This is but a part—

KIT: Harry, no—

HARRY: —The other pages lie in my chamber down the hall and my servant below hath more.

ACTOR: *(As* DINGLEBERRY. *Craftily, pointing at* KIT*)* Ah, wouldst send me astray. Leave not this room, I charge thee! Obedience will be sorely punished!

*(*DINGLEBERRY *dashes out.* HARRY *dashes to the window and throws it open.)*

KIT: Harry, must thou assist this worthy fool?

HARRY: I am assisting thee! Make thy escape!

KIT: I'll not clamber down the trellis like an adulterer.

HARRY: You must! Thy manuscript is confiscate—what will follow?

KIT: Her Majesty will read it and enjoy.

HARRY: Art certain? The rack and pyre could be thy fate.

KIT: She's erudite—and liketh me well.

HARRY: Depend not on that, as thou hast told me.

KIT: And she liketh thee well. Will you speak to her?

HARRY: I said I can, but cannot guarantee—what should I say?

KIT: It matters not, if you say it. Thou art in particular favor presently. If thou lovest me.

HARRY: I do—I will—and gladly too!
(Practically pushing him out the window)
But better thou shouldst flee!

KIT: No, I shall rely on thee. And on my Queen.

(The ACTOR, *as* DINGLEBERRY, *bursts in, virtually apoplectic.)*

ACTOR: *(As* DINGLEBERRY. *Waving many pages)* 'Tis pious and most blasphemetical! *(Pointing at* KIT*)* Infidel! Thou art hermetical in the extreme!

KIT: Everyone's a critic.

ACTOR: *(As* DINGLEBERRY*)* These profundities burn my eyes ere I read them!

KIT: Thou readst?

ACTOR: *(As* DINGLEBERRY*)* And very well—dost poke fun at me? I am very disrespected in my profession, sir.

KIT: And rightly so.

ACTOR: *(As* DINGLEBERRY. *Smiling)* Good. *(Frowning)* But I'll not be flattered.

KIT: 'Tis impossible.

ACTOR: *(As* DINGLEBERRY*)* Thou art arrested, poet. Come with me.

HARRY: What is the charge?

ACTOR: *(As* DINGLEBERRY*)* Hermetical writings most devout! *(Grabbing* KIT*)* Shalt defend thy pieties before the Privy Council.

KIT: *(As* DINGLEBERRY *drags him off)* Forget not thy promise!

HARRY: I'll see her presently.

KIT: Remember, Harry, I love thee well.

HARRY: And I thee.

KIT: Lead on, o perspicacious constable.

ACTOR: *(As* DINGLEBERRY*)* Dost mock me, still? But I shall mock thee as thou burnst, dissenter, and watch thy fame go up in flame.

*(*DINGLEBERRY *drags* KIT *out, leaving* HARRY *behind.)*

END OF ACT ONE

ACT TWO

(Lights up on the interior of a room above Eleanor Bull's tavern. This room could very much resemble the room in Southampton House, with the addition of a bed. The ACTOR *drags* HARRY *into the room.* HARRY *carries a fairly large bag and the* ACTOR *a satchel.)*

HARRY: You cannot keep me from him!

ACTOR: One step toward London and I'll cut off the foot that takes it.

HARRY: Then will thy fears be bootless indeed!

ACTOR: 'Tis for thine own surety we've fled town. You agreed to come—

HARRY: I've changed my mind—

ACTOR: Thy name and Marlowe's must not be uttered in the same breath.

HARRY: I'll get an audience with the Queen—

ACTOR: Hast seen a heretic burn?

HARRY: No.

ACTOR: 'Tis a scientific lesson in heats and currents. Greenwood lets them die of smoke, which is much kinder. Dry wood incinerates the sinner to death, but overstacking smothers the flames and draws out the torment. In eighty-nine Francis Kett's blackened, blistered lips cried, "More wood!" but the executioner carefully stoked the embers for the longest, loudest show.

HARRY: If need be, he'll go bravely to it.

ACTOR: Aye, but will you?

HARRY: Like Joan of Arc.

ACTOR: Model not thy life on enemies of the crown.

HARRY: I am none, and therefore have no fear. *(Pulls out pages of manuscript)* See what I have salvaged.

ACTOR: Wherefore do I protect thee? Thou hast brought the damning pages with thee!

HARRY: Thou seest I love his play. Let me go to him. Art thou afeared to see the competition through?

ACTOR: Be not so fond.

HARRY: Then I shall hawk the parchments in the street.

ACTOR: *(Forcibly halting him)* You'll not go forth!

HARRY: Canst keep watch all night?

ACTOR: No, but—

HARRY: I'll stay. But you must play with me.

ACTOR: Twere better I played all the parts.

HARRY: The play was writ for me.

ACTOR: Vanity, vanity.

HARRY: "Vanity" cries the actor! Dost hate the play because it doth not flatter thee? Thou art Judas to a T.

ACTOR: 'Twas Thomas Kyd confessed his name.

HARRY: Thou doth play the traitor well— 'twas all I meant. *(Pulling costumes out of the bag)* I've brought our costumes and stage properties. *(Proffering the bag)* I read ahead a bit, and guessed the rest—we know the ending of the tale.

ACTOR: I hate prop-heavy shows. Ow! *(Pulls a crown of thorns from the bag)* 'Tis painfully real for the stage. *(Pulls out a dead rat with a string attached)* Aagh! Where are there rats in scripture?

HARRY: In the next scene. *(Dumps out the rest of the bag's contents: two more stringed rats and the potion vial.)*

HARRY: I bought them from a coachman in the livery and strung them up myself. *(He drops his purse on the table and arranges the rats on the floor.)*

ACTOR: You bought rats? Art clearly unaccustomed to the theatre. Real rats will rot and spoil the scene. Bits of fur and leather, cleverly constructed—stage rats—are much more to the purpose.

HARRY: Is there a rat shortage in London? For each performance there'll be a fresh supply. Now study thy part—'tis a goodly speech and thou art alone on stage.

ACTOR: A soliloquy? *(Takes the pages and begins memorizing.)*

HARRY: My attempts to discover the Biblical basis for this scene have proven singularly unsuccessful, but perhaps 'tis what enchants me.

ACTOR: Done.

HARRY: Most excellent! Sit here.

(HARRY positions the ACTOR on the floor surrounded by the rats and hands him the potion vial.)

HARRY: Oh—thy hump!

(HARRY gives the ACTOR his hump. The ACTOR dons it but is not pleased to take direction from an amateur.)

HARRY: Thou mayst begin.

(The ACTOR merely glares at HARRY.)

HARRY: At thy pleasure.

ACTOR: (*As* JUDAS. *After taking a very deliberate moment.*)
Hosanna! cried the stones o'er which he rode
Into Jerusalem, while waving palms
And scatter'd garments strow'd his kingly path.
'Tis the Messiah! shouted every soul
He raiseth up the dead, wilt raise the Jews
In holy war against the Roman scourge!
And I, unthinking, engined this quaint fraud.
(*Indicating the rats.*)
Five pernicious rodents, greed-gnawing rats,
Hours ago did sup upon this draught,
The self-same drink young John did quaff withal.
'Twere five dead vermin rotting on the floor
And neither dog, nor cat, nor starving bairn
Hath ventured here to dine upon this feast.
Yet only three remain. Where are the two?
Aha! I spy a resurrecting rat!

(HARRY, *somewhat out of view, tweaks the string attached
to one rat, making the rat wiggle.*)

ACTOR: (*As* JUDAS. *To the wiggling rat*)
Whoso believes in me, though he were dead,
Yet will he live.

(HARRY *drags the rat as* JUDAS *tries to stomp it.*)

ACTOR: (*As* JUDAS) But not for very long!

(HARRY *drags the rat safely away from* JUDAS.)

ACTOR: (*As* JUDAS)
I am bewilder'd, and confuse these rats
With men I loathe, for loathe them I do both!
My murder turned a miracle, and made
A man a god. When poison John consumed
There presently through all his veins did run
A cold and drowsy humor; for no pulse
Did keep his native progress, but surceas'd;
No warmth, no breath did testify he lived;
Each part, depriv'd of supple government,

Did, stiff and stark and cold, appear like death,
And in this borrowed likeness of shrunk death—

(HARRY *"resurrects" another rat.*)

ACTOR: *(As* JUDAS)
He did continue five and twenty hours—
And then awake as from a pleasant sleep!

(JUDAS *tries to stomp the second rat but it gets away.
Squeaks are supplied by* HARRY.)

ACTOR: *(As* JUDAS)
Pretended poison! Counterfeit of death!
Hast surely crowned a counterfeited king!
Astride an ass, an ass himself he rode,
With John beside him—proof!—at his right hand.
And where ranked I in this poor passing show?
Behind the ass atripping on its dung!
(Smiling)
Wherefore did I protect him from himself?
No longer shall I bate his o'erblown pride
Nor stay the overreaching of his grasp,
But puff up pride with poison promise and
Convince him of his godly attributes.
Hosannas loud have caught the Roman ear
And Pharisees and scribes his progress trace;
Shall make him Messianic in his mind
And let him doom himself with outward show.
(The third rat "revives".)
The miracle—beloved John's new breath—
Shall for our new Messiah knell his death.

(JUDAS *enthusiastically stomps the rat to death.* HARRY
stares, repulsed.)

HARRY: You stomped my prop.

ACTOR: *(As himself. Breathing hard as he takes off the
hump)* It felt right.

HARRY: I said 'tis goodly writ.

ACTOR: But didst thou like the playing?

HARRY: 'Twas natural because 'twas writ for thee.

ACTOR: Stop saying that!

HARRY: Not five minutes past I heard thee utter "Wherefore do I protect?" and then as Judas quote thyself. He knows thee.

ACTOR: (*Angrily balling up one of the pages*) He is a fiend and hath ensnared thee!

HARRY: (*Rescuing the page*) He is himself ensnared, and is trying even now to tear the net. But you've ensnared me as well—I've been waiting for thy latest sonnet with no little patience.

ACTOR: (*Producing pages from his satchel*) That's because I've written thee three.

HARRY: (*Toying with the string of the stomped rat*) I'll read them if you'll swab up this mess. The hostess will otherwise give us the boot as you gave it to the rat.

ACTOR: (*As they trade string for pages*) These are heartfelt, and not designed for Burghley, but for thee.

HARRY: For that I thank thee, but think not that you'll distract me from London with mere rhymes. Thinkest thou he will plead well before the Privy Council?

ACTOR: If he can check his arrogance—'tis doubtful that he will—then he may not burn.

(HARRY *settles down to read as the* ACTOR *busies himself with the unpleasant task of cleaning up the dead rats. The lights shift so that a portion of the stage is isolated.* KIT *appears in the light as if before the Privy Council.*)

KIT: Worthy gentlemen, you know me well. If not by sight, by word, for members of this council have many times seen—and praised—such dramas as *Tamburlaine, The Jew of Malta,* and *Doctor Faustus.* They are mine, and I am theirs. The Scythian shepherd, the

wronged Jew, and the misunderstood and conjuring
scholar are in some wise me. I am, of course, neither
shepherd, Jew nor conjurer—but stand outside
society's bounds as they do. As poets must. You have
in your possession scant, scratchy notes—not even
scenes as yet—fragments from yet another play. 'Tis
the tale of another who took men to task for who they
were, and who they claimed to be, and shamed them
for their sins. But loved them still, and offered them
salvation. He stood outside, offending strictured law
and angering men. As gods must. The snatches you've
compiled, dramatic scraps, sow the seeds of conflict,
doubt, and disorder in the play—and in your hearts.
For how shall drama lead sans questions pulling
us along? The questions you've seen sown are dire,
dreadful, you think perhaps heretical.

(The lights begin to change so that KIT *is in the room with*
HARRY *and the* ACTOR *recounting his testimony.* HARRY
and the ACTOR *complete their activities and listen to him.)*

KIT: What better drama? The mysteries of the universe,
of God, are surely worthy of the stage! How better
may we educate the populace than by demonstrating
heresies, then damning them? For you have read Act
One, scene one, a soliloquy from Act Two, bits of Three
and Four—but not Act Five. And as a wise young man
once said, how shall we judge a play before the bows?
Doth not the end illume all that goes before? Act Five
discourses on divinity, as it pertains to God…and to
our Queen. Wilt condemn before the resolution? So
far I am successful—hast made thee ponder. So hear it
out—the play may yet prove God beyond all proof.

*(*KIT *looks at the other two for approval.)*

HARRY: How could they else but set thee free?

ACTOR: Especially when a wise young man hath posted
bail.

KIT: Thank heaven you did, or I would never have found thee. 'Twas hard to picture thee in an inn in Deptford Strand.

HARRY: 'Twas his choice.

KIT: Which dost thou protect, my lord or me?

HARRY: *(To* KIT*)* Protect—his very word! *(To the* ACTOR*)* He's hit on it again! The poet's winning, player!

ACTOR: You've but delayed your suicide by that speech! For certainly you dream of immolation as you write these words!

KIT: And thee of spiriting him away!

ACTOR: To protect him, yes!

KIT: Who's protecting him from thee?

*(*ACTOR *pushes* KIT *with the rolled pages.)*

ACTOR: I'll not see him staked beside me on the pyre!

HARRY: Gentlemen—if I may call thee that—!

KIT: *(Reaching for the parchment)* Tear not the page!

ACTOR: *(Keeping it away from* KIT*)* 'Tis not the page, nor phrase I fault. 'Tis in whose mouths they're put!

KIT: *(Pursuing)* But thou dost mouth these words so well!

ACTOR: The words doth charm—and therefore the more evilly deceive. Dissevered from this filthy, lying play— *(Tears out a few lines of verse)* —They're angelic, lofty thoughts—much as you used to write—

KIT: *(Lunging at the* ACTOR*)* Tear them not!

HARRY: Calm thyselves! We'll get kicked out!

ACTOR: *(Gleefully tearing more)* —I'm setting worthy phrases free!

KIT: *(Grabbing ahold of the pages)* I am their master!

ACTOR: And I their slave? I think not. They're my offspring as well—you must trust me to give them life.

(A tug-o-war ensues.)

HARRY: Rend not thy child between thee!

KIT: Thank you, worthy Solomon!

ACTOR: Solomon!? This boy you told me was not wise?!

HARRY: What?

KIT: *(Forgetting the manuscript; going for the* ACTOR'*s throat)* Thou hast too heartily sucked up thy role, Judas!

(Surrendering the manuscript, the ACTOR *dashes for the door.)*

ACTOR: If thou art Christ, you've doomed yourself to die!

(The ACTOR *disappears out the door, but* KIT *does not pursue.* HARRY *slumps.* KIT *watches* HARRY.*)*

KIT: 'Tis true.

*(*HARRY *tries to wave him away.)*

KIT: I did once doubt thy erudition—thy—

HARRY: I know what erudition means! You need not translate.

KIT: *(Touching* HARRY'*s hair)* I first admired thy hair— how could I not? *(Touching him other places)* And then thy grace—

HARRY: *(Pushing him away)* But most of all my fortune—get thee gone!

KIT: Oh, shall we wrestle—? *(Tearing off his own shirt)* — Like the Greeks?

HARRY: *(Pushing against* KIT *as he advances)* Only get thee gone if I'm a fool!

KIT: I said not that.

HARRY: But I'll be one no more—at least no more thine!

KIT: Hast cut off a very pretty speech!

(KIT *tears off* HARRY's *shirt.*)

HARRY: *(Grabbing his shirt back)* Too many pretty speeches, pretty falsehoods, hath bewitched my brain!

KIT: Stay still enough to listen—

(HARRY *and* KIT *wrestle.*)

HARRY: I was right to flee thee!

KIT: I at one time loved thy money more than thee—

HARRY: Parasite!

KIT: And thought thy innocence thy largest virtue—

HARRY: Get off!

KIT: But thy comely face is a mere mask, concealing—

HARRY: Concealing!

KIT: Let me get it out—it's good! Concealing thy true beauty, thy noble soul.

HARRY: False flattery!

KIT: Flattery my arse! Thou hast changed my play!

HARRY: What?

KIT: When first conceived, my play was blasphemous to the last stroke, a paper demon born of my belief…in naught. But it lies stillborn, dumb—

HARRY: Dumb—that's how you think of me—!

KIT: Before I knew thee…and believed in thee. I've seen into thy heart and redrafted my scenario with a new ending. I've never altered a line for anyone before. Ask the actor.

HARRY: But…what did I do?

KIT: Thy offer of intercession with the Queen. 'Tis dangerous…and noble.

HARRY: I have not done it yet.

KIT: What I told the Privy Council was no lie—let's see how things turn out.

(KIT *has pinned* HARRY; *both are panting.*)

KIT: In life as well as drama. As thou hast—wisely—said. Art not curious to see how this turns out?

HARRY: (*Their eyes meet; after a moment.*) The wrestling match or play?

KIT: I have won the match. Didst expect more end than this?

HARRY: (*Again, the staring match and pause*) The play.

KIT: (*Jumping up*) These pages that our Judas hath abused, I wrote before I discovered thy retreat. Shall we play them in these costumes?

HARRY: (*Almost shyly producing the costumes*) I brought those we used before.

KIT: (*Pleased, he dons his drape; so does* HARRY.*) Excellent! The scene starts with thy speech explaining deviation—

HARRY: What?

KIT: —From the scriptures—'tis a goodly writer's speech. Pray begin.

HARRY: (*As* JOHN. *Writing*)
"And then he did cry loudly, John come forth!
At once he that was dead came forth—" Fie, fie!
'Tis true, but doth it seem fair honest that
The writer of these words is he who rose?
'Twill never be believ'd! All poets glorify
Themselves—'tis widely known—and thus my words
Be cast in suspect light. The miracle
Took place, but I cannot the subject be.
I'll make it up! Create a man to die
And live again. Poetical his name

Should be, and mirror his strange tale, yet not
Too otherworldly sound. Ah—Lazarus—
Now there's a goodly name. It meaneth "helped
By God." Yes. "Lazarus come forth," he cried.
(Writes with great energy)

ACTOR: *(As* JUDAS. *Enters wearing the hump)* Art
scrawling lies—?

HARRY: *(As* JOHN) Oh, get thee from my sight,
Thou gav'st me poison. Dangerous fellow, hence!
Breathe not where true disciples are.

ACTOR: *(As* JUDAS) What's this?
I never bid thee taste of that fell vial.

HARRY: *(As* JOHN)
E'en so, thy honey-rich persuasion made
The liquor sweeter grow until I drank.

ACTOR: *(As* JUDAS) Thou saidst thou weren't in love.

HARRY: *(As* JOHN) Nor never was!

KIT: *(As* JESUS. *Enters, wearing the drape.)*
Be not contentious, gentle friends, but love
And trust each other—as thou know'st I teach.

ACTOR: *(As* JUDAS. *Bowing slightly)*
Belov'd of God. Thy truth we do revere.
(Embraces JOHN, *aside to him.)*
Taint not his miracle.

HARRY: *(As* JOHN) But you—he gave—

KIT: *(As* JESUS)
What art thou stammering to say, dear friend?

HARRY: *(As* JOHN) Oh—nothing. Not a word.

ACTOR: *(As* JUDAS) We argued, Lord, about a prophecy.

KIT: *(As* JESUS) Pray, which?

ACTOR: *(As* JUDAS) Hosea said, "Return unto the Lord,
In two days' time He will our souls revive.

On the third day the Lord will raise us up,
And we shall live in His sight." Now John took this
To mean forsooth that the Messiah reigns
By cheating churlish death and rising free
Of Earthly bounds and leading men to life.

KIT: (*As* JESUS. *To* JOHN)
Dost claim the orb and scepter as our king?

HARRY: (*As* JOHN)
No, no—'twas thee that rais'd me up from death.
I argued not 'gainst that, nor for myself.

KIT: (*As* JESUS) Then how?

HARRY: (*As* JOHN) I must confess—

ACTOR: (*As* JUDAS) He framed it thus:
His resurrection prov'd thy pow'r o'er death,
But as Messiah, thou—

KIT: (*As* JESUS) 'Twas God-giv'n pow'r—

ACTOR: (*As* JUDAS) `Struth, it was. It is. But let me not
Claim title to another man's wise words.

(JOHN *just looks at* JUDAS, *confused.*)

ACTOR: Wast eloquent in the extreme just now.

HARRY: (*As* JOHN) I don't—what did—?

ACTOR: (*As* JUDAS) Be not so shy!

KIT: (*As* JESUS) Expound!

ACTOR: (*As* JUDAS)
Forgive me my impatience with his tongue;
His modesty belies his deeper thought.
Most simply put, he reasoned that one death
And resurrection more wouldst vouch for thee.

KIT: (*As* JESUS) Wouldst true Messiah prove?

HARRY: (*As* JOHN) What?

KIT: (*As* JESUS) Whose?

ACTOR: (*As* JUDAS) But thine.

HARRY: (*As* JOHN) No, hold—!

ACTOR: (*As* JUDAS) —Cried I, how can this be? But John
Did chide me thus—dost doubt my miracle?
Do I not live? So could he die and live.

(JOHN *cannot speak.*)

KIT: (*As* JESUS) 'Tis hard—

HARRY: (*As* JOHN) I know—

KIT: (*As* JESUS) —But wise.

ACTOR: (*As* JUDAS) I argued 'gainst—

KIT: (*As* JESUS) Dispute it not. It comes as if from God.
Dost know thy scripture well.

ACTOR: (*As* JUDAS) Thou shouldst, he said,
Be absolute for death: either death or life
Shall thereby be the sweeter. Reason thus with life:
If I do lose thee, I do lose a thing
That none but fools would keep. A breath thou art,
Servile to all the skyey influences,
That dost this habitation where thou keepst
Hourly afflict. Merely, thou art death's fool,
For him thou laborst by thy flight to shun,
And yet runst toward him still. What's yet in this
That bears the name of life? Yet in this life
Lie hid moe thousand deaths; yet death we fear
That makes these odds all even.

KIT: (*As* JESUS. *To* JOHN, *astonished*)
Saidst thou this?

(JOHN *shakes his head no, then yes.*)

ACTOR: (*As* JUDAS)
Couldst have a finer author of thy words?

KIT: (*As* JESUS) Come let us dine together and debate
Fulfillment of these pithy prophecies.

(JESUS *and* JUDAS *go out.* JOHN *hesitates.*)

HARRY: (*As* JOHN)
I am undone! I've spoken witty words
And wise through that deceiver's facile mouth,
Yet I do fear where they may lead my Lord.
My protestations null'd before I speak,
For I dare not to gainsay miracles.
That which I drank, I wonder could it be
A certain stuff, which, being ta'en, would cease
The present pow'r of life, but in short time
All offices of nature should again
Do their due functions? Shall I intervene
Betwixt my Lord and cold, obdurate death
By stifling newborn hopes that give him breath?

HARRY: (*As himself, breaking character*) John's love is not unmixed.

KIT: (*Returning, as himself, laughing*) And very droll.

HARRY: (*Disconcerted*) But I am moved by his dilemma—to tell a truth he fears or hold his tongue and perhaps condemn a man to death.

(HARRY *and* KIT *remove the drape and dress.*)

KIT: I am moved as well—to laughter.

HARRY: Thou art cold to thine own words. 'Tis surely not a comedy.

KIT: Comedies end with marriage, tragedies with death.

HARRY: And death, we know, concludes this tale. The passion of our Lord could ne'er be comic.

KIT: But 'tis John's passion, not Christ's.

(*There is a knock at the door.*)

HARRY: Who knows we're here?

KIT: Be not so pigeon-hearted. Let's see.

(KIT *opens the door. The* ACTOR *comes in wearing the moustache and brown wig, as* TOM. *His fingers are still bandaged and he's still twitchy.)*

KIT: Tommy!

ACTOR: *(As* TOM) Thou art perhaps too easily found, yet I am glad to see thee.

HARRY: Come in, quickly, and shut the door. How fares thy hand?

ACTOR: *(As* TOM. *Gingerly pulling his hand away from* HARRY*)* I thank your lordship for asking—but please don't touch. I've come from London.

KIT: What hast thou heard? Walsingham would not see me for a fit of pique.

ACTOR: *(As* TOM) I saw him. Her Majesty is not favorably disposed.

KIT: I spoke so well...I thought...

ACTOR: *(As* TOM) No decision will be rendered till thy trial, but—

HARRY & KIT: *(Simultaneously)* I'll [Wilt] speak to her. [?] *(They both laugh.)*

KIT: Thank you, Harry.

HARRY: *(Heading for the door)* Right now. I'm off to London.

KIT: You need not rush. *(Hands him a page)* Here, take this.

ACTOR: *(As* TOM) Must rush indeed.

(Both HARRY *and* KIT *look quite worried.* HARRY *disappears.)*

ACTOR: *(As* TOM) Do you trust him?

KIT: With my life.

ACTOR: (As TOM) Thou hast. (Pulls out a parchment.) Thy actor friend seeks to join our mystery.

KIT: (Grabbing the parchment) Wilt call himself a poet? Let's see.

ACTOR: (As TOM) 'Tis time for flight, not words.

KIT: 'Tis always time for words. (Scanning the sonnet) Not bad, for an actor. At least he hath not slandered me. He still reveres my verse.

ACTOR: (As TOM) 'Tis not of thee.

KIT: 'Tis of Harry—and of me!

ACTOR: (As TOM) Thou swell-head! The world thinks not of thee both night and day!

KIT: Doth mention Faustus—spirits. 'Tis of me. And of our contest for Southampton's favor. But more alarming still— 'tis in past tense! Doth claim the prize!?

ACTOR: (As TOM) Methinks he hath against thee worked.

KIT: But The Beloved Disciple shall yet win me mine! I'll hire a troop of actors to perform the play aright.

ACTOR: (As TOM. Getting up to leave) Thou hast lost the queen, art charged with heresy, and thou'lt have no patron! (Taking KIT by the hand, he winces.) Come with me to France—escape the stake.

KIT: Harry will save me. I'll convince him yet. And, Tommy, we mustn't lose our faith in queens.

(The ACTOR as TOM smiles, but is unconvinced. He hugs KIT warmly and leaves. KIT sits down and begins to write. On another part of the stage, in a discrete area of light, HARRY, with a lantern, reads the page KIT handed him. As before, HARRY's movements while reading mirror or relate to KIT's while writing.)

HARRY: *(Reading* JOHN's *speech)*
It is the cause, it is the cause, my soul;
Let me not name it to you, you chaste stars,
It is the cause. Yet I'll not shed his blood,
Nor scar that whiter skin of his than snow,
And smooth as monumental alablaster.
Yet he must die, or suspect truth reveal.
Was I reborn of witchcraft or of God?
And even if he raised me from the dead,
How should he raise himself once he is cold?
I can with tortured silence snuff his life.
If I quench thee, thou flaming minister,
I can again thy former light restore,
Should I repent me; but once put out thy light,
Thou cunningst pattern of excelling nature,
I know not where is that Promethean heat
That can thy light relume. When I have pluck'd thy
    rose,
I cannot give it vital growth again,
It needs must wither.
(He looks puzzled.)
Why gav'st me this?

(While KIT *writes with great energy,* HARRY's *area of light expands to reveal* QUEEN ELIZABETH *hunched in a chair. She is a stunningly dressed, but aging monarch played by the* ACTOR. *When he sees her,* HARRY *falls to his knees.)*

ACTOR: *(As* ELIZABETH*)* Rise, Southampton. Come hither.

*(*HARRY *goes to her. She strokes his cheek.)*

ACTOR: *(As* ELIZABETH*)* Dost come to plead?

HARRY: To bleed? Your Majesty, I hope not!

ACTOR: *(As* ELIZABETH*)* Not bleed—

HARRY: Oh, I thought you said—

ACTOR: *(As* ELIZABETH*)* Plead.

HARRY: I'm sorry. Yes. I do. Come to plead, I mean.

(She waits. He just stares for a moment.)

ACTOR: *(As* ELIZABETH*)* For whom?

HARRY: Thou knowst I come to plead—must surely know for whom.

ACTOR: *(As* ELIZABETH. *Producing a number of parchment pages)* This poet…and blasphemer.

HARRY: 'Tis a most religious play, Your Majesty!

ACTOR: *(As* ELIZABETH*)* In subject, not in sense.

HARRY: Hast read the end?

ACTOR: *(As* ELIZABETH*)* Nay, but 'tis predictable. We know the scripture—why write more?

HARRY: Perhaps the author aims to illuminate the humanity in scripture.

ACTOR: *(As* ELIZABETH*)* We hardly need Our Lord dragged through the guttered streets.

HARRY: Dost miss the subtlety, methinks.

ACTOR: *(As* ELIZABETH*)* Thou thinkst! Hast kept company with university wits perhaps too long. Thy sweet character hath altered, dear boy. Thou thinkst!

HARRY: What of the very language? Admirest not that? The cleverness of phrase, the turns of speech, conceits, similes, and spritely painted scenes—art not in awe?

ACTOR: *(As* ELIZABETH*)* In awe of his audacity.

HARRY: Ist all? Didst not find it comic? The water-walking?

ACTOR: *(As* ELIZABETH*)* 'Tis true I laughed—indeed, I tittered like a schoolgirl at the false miracles—and took my guilty pleasure at the tricks.

HARRY: The feeding of the five thousand.

ACTOR: *(As* ELIZABETH*)* And the rats—most droll!

HARRY: The deadly love potion! Wast not a quaint device?

ACTOR: *(As* ELIZABETH. *Smiling)* An amusing parody of convention.

HARRY: Didst enjoy the writer naming Lazarus?

ACTOR: *(As* ELIZABETH*)* Satirizing his own trade. He knows it well.

HARRY: And in the tragic vein—wert moved?

ACTOR: *(As* ELIZABETH*)* My heart twisted like a tear-wrung kerchief for lovestruck John's travails.

HARRY: *(Holds out his hand)* The resurrection of John by Christ's trembling hand?

ACTOR: *(As* ELIZABETH. *She takes his hand.)* 'Twas a tender scene. Lovely.

HARRY: And o'er shadowing all, we know that Christ will by play's end be dead.

ACTOR: *(As* ELIZABETH*)* And live again.

HARRY: Although the end is still unwrit, given what has gone before, what metaphor empowers resurrection?

ACTOR: *(As* ELIZABETH*)* Love?

HARRY: Indeed! Love of God—resembling in his metaphor, England's love for you!

ACTOR: *(As* ELIZABETH. *Beaming)* For me.

HARRY: A triumphant tribute!

ACTOR: *(As* ELIZABETH*)* Ah, clever poet. *(Her brow suddenly darkens, she drops his hand.)* Jesus Christ died virgin! 'Tis a fact I will not permit disputed.

HARRY: No—'tis but thy interpretation! Cannot be his intent!

ACTOR: (*As* ELIZABETH) This with Our Lord's sodomy toys—couldst be more baldly clear?

HARRY: I saw that love as—but—thou like'st the play!

ACTOR: (*As* ELIZABETH) Indeed. There's much to praise—which condemns the play the more! Though I may like it privately, I am not a private person, but an actor, and must act for public good. The questions raised by this play, this poetical sacrilege, are—to use thy word—too subtle for the groundlings, too clever, indeed, for court. 'Twould confuse, foment disorder. 'Tis treasonous.

HARRY: 'Tis a capital charge, Your Majesty.

(*She just stares at him.*)

HARRY: Remember, my lady, he served thee.

ACTOR: (*As* ELIZABETH) He that will forget God will also forget his benefactors.

HARRY: (*Kneeling again*) If not for him, dear lady, then for me.

ACTOR: (*As* ELIZABETH. *Stroking his hair*) Why dost thou plead for him? He is but a poet and hath not blood.

HARRY: I love him.

ACTOR: (*As* ELIZABETH) Thou art young and knowst not how to choose thy friends. (*She strokes his shoulder, perhaps squeezing it.*) 'Tis noised about he hath succumbed to the sodomitical vice as well as atheism— both capital crimes. Better thou art well away.

HARRY: My love for him is noble, Majesty.

ACTOR: (*As* ELIZABETH. *Looking into his eyes, stroking his cheek*) Its nobility cometh from thee, not from him. Mingle not thy noble passion with his baseness. (*Now with both hands on him*) Thou'rt made for higher things.

HARRY: Then, there is no help?

ACTOR: *(As* ELIZABETH*)* Indeed, thou canst help me.

HARRY: Would that help him?

ACTOR: *(As* ELIZABETH*)* In a sense. Dost understand how he hath offended, not only me, but every living creature? His play, however brilliantly it shines, casts doubt on God as we know Him. Its written form doth also confuse—ist an amusing tragedy or a somber comedy? Poetry and culture—the muses themselves— are assaulted. And what sayeth he of government? Judas urges rebellion. 'Tis intolerable. Religion, culture, government are one. *(Indicating herself)* An holy trinity. Offending one doth undermine the three—and he hath aimed at all. Artistic heresy and sedition are cut from the same soiled cloth.

HARRY: He meant no harm.

ACTOR: *(As* ELIZABETH*)* Indeed he did. *(Rattling the pages)* I am Jesus Christ, know ye not that?

HARRY: How may I help…thee?

ACTOR: *(As* ELIZABETH. *Caressing* HARRY*)* Marlowe hath committed suicide with his pen. The rack and then the stake are his destiny—he knows that, I am certain. But *Tamburlaine* was popular, and *Faustus, The Jew,* and *Edward II* as well. Tying him atop the purifying faggots would only incense the mob that loves him. He knows that he must die. 'Twere of his own hand, 'twere better. *(Stands to leave)* Thou canst reveal to him the light, and honor me, and save thyself.

*(*ELIZABETH *kisses* HARRY *and disappears.* HARRY *is stunned.)*

HARRY: My God, that woman hath balls!

(Gradually the lights shift to illuminate the entire stage so that HARRY *and* KIT *are in the same area.* KIT *finishes writing with a triumphal flourish and regards the trembling* HARRY *with some impatience.)*

KIT: I gather from thy mute trembling she did not choose to sponsor a production.

HARRY: Thy good was her concern.

KIT: My good!? Never have I been *good*! Great, perhaps, but never mundane good. Aught else?

HARRY: Much about thy fragments she doth like—

KIT: Yes, speak—

HARRY: *(Thinking quickly)* —And desireth the play's conclusion before thou see'st the Privy Council again.

KIT: *(Delighted, holding up the manuscript)* 'Tis here. Shall we to it?

HARRY: *(Reaching for the manuscript)* Let me see.

KIT: So hot! So hasty! What's here that you desire so urgently?

HARRY: Just the end.

KIT: Cool thy ardor for the final act until we're three once more. Without our Judas, this tale has no end.

ACTOR: *(Entering with food)* The food here stinks—I've brought up the best I could.

KIT: On cue, Iscariot! Don hump and scowl, thou villain—her highness wants the ending of the play.

ACTOR: First let's eat.

KIT: I cannot—I'm in the service of the Queen.

ACTOR: 'Twas all she said? No more?

KIT: *(Passing them pages)* Thy final chance to prove thy worth—our contest nears its conclusion as well.

HARRY: I desire the end as much as she. Then I shall judge.

KIT: *(Passing out the costumes)* Act well, then, friend. For I have writ my best. *(To HARRY)* Disrobe and don full costume. I must wash thy feet.

(HARRY *reluctantly takes off his clothes and puts on the* *dress.* KIT *produces a basin full of water. Annoyed, the* ACTOR *dons his hump.*)

ACTOR: This is the last I'll act this part. It makes me ill.

KIT: Think how thy ill performance sickens me.

(*The* ACTOR *looks hurt.*)

KIT: 'Tis not ill. Thou hast thy grandest speeches in this scene. I have, like Cana's wedding, saved the good wine for last. (*To* HARRY) Art done?

HARRY: Nearly.

KIT: 'Tis the scene of a great reckoning in a little room. (*Indicating a spot on the manuscript*) Let us commence here. Time is not ours, but the Queen's.

(KIT *sits at* HARRY's *feet and begins washing* HARRY's *bare* *foot. The* ACTOR *moves away from the scene, cutting up and* *eating food with the knife. Reluctantly,* HARRY *begins.*)

HARRY: (*As* JOHN)
Aye, but to die, and go we know not where;
To lie in cold obstruction, and to rot;
This sensible warm motion to become
A kneaded clod; and the delighted spirit
To bathe in fiery floods, or to reside
In thrilling region of thick-ribbed ice;
To be imprison'd in the viewless winds
And blown with restless violence round about
The pendant world; or to be worse than worst
Of those that lawless and incertain thought
Imagine howling—'tis too horrible!
The weariest and most loathed worldly life
That age, ache, penury, and imprisonment
Can lay on nature is a paradise
To what we fear of death.

KIT: (*As* JESUS. *Washing*) Fear not, fear not.
For I shall raise me up as I did thee.

HARRY: (*As* JOHN)
Dost know how thou didst cause me so to rise?

KIT: (*As* JESUS)
With faith in God, who maketh all things true.

HARRY: (*As* JOHN) Art certain? Could another agency
Have called me hither? Or perhaps my death
Was but a picture or a mumming ruse?

KIT: (*As* JESUS)
Thou wert as dead and breathless as a stone.

HARRY: (*As* JOHN) I seemed so.

KIT: (*As* JESUS) I mourned o'er thy cold corse.

HARRY: (*As* JOHN)
Dost know what caus'd me suddenly to die?

KIT: (*As* JESUS) Thou saidst a fever flush upon thy brow.

HARRY: (*As* JOHN)
But ere that fever took me from this world
I tasted of a bitter drink from Greece
That Judas gave and bid me not to sip.

KIT: (*As* JESUS)
Why didst he give? And why didst thou it drink?

HARRY: (*As* JOHN) For love of thee.

KIT: (*As* JESUS) Didst die for me?

HARRY: (*As* JOHN) Indeed.
Before I took the fatal draught I died
Each hour that I my passion stifled.
Until thou took my hand and bid me wake
I never liv'd but suffered want of thee.
(*Produces vial*)
This potion Judas claimed could seal a kiss
Could only steal thy love by killing me—
Or worse, produce a death-like sleep from whence
I woke to find a miracle proclaimed.

(JESUS *begins pouring wine.*)

KIT: (*As* JESUS)
Have not we proven since we bought your life
That love need not resort to alchemy.

(*They stare at each other a moment while* JESUS *pours.* JOHN *looks up.*)

HARRY: (*As* JOHN)
The moon shines bright. In such a night as this,
When the sweet wind did gently kiss the trees,
And they did make no noise, in such a night
Troilus methinks mounted the Troyan walls,
And sigh'd his soul toward the Grecian tents,
Where Cressid lay that night.

KIT: (*As* JESUS. *Picking up wineglasses, as if to leave*)
In such a night,
Different from all other nights, we know
And we remember why we are the chosen.

HARRY: (*As* JOHN. *Taking one of the full glasses.*)
Ere we th' eleven join in our
Unleaven feast, swear to our love for me.

KIT: (*As* JESUS)
My friend, by yonder blessed moon I vow,
That tips with silver all the fruit-tree tops—

HARRY: (*As* JOHN)
O, swear not by the moon, th' inconstant moon,
That monthly changes in her circled orb,
Lest that thy love prove likewise variable.

KIT: (*As* JESUS) If I profane with my unworthiest hand
This holy shrine, the gentle fine is this,
My lips, two blushing pilgrims, ready stand
To smooth that rough touch with a tender kiss.

(*They kiss.*)

KIT: *(As* JESUS*)*
Thus from my lips, by thine, my sin is purged.

HARRY: *(As* JOHN*)*
Then have my lips the sin that they have took.

KIT: *(As* JESUS*)*
Sin from my lips? O trespass sweetly urg'd!
Give me my sin again.

(They kiss again.)

HARRY: *(As* JOHN. *Extremely aroused but equally
uncomfortable.)*
You kiss by th' book.

*(*JESUS *leans in for another kiss, but* HARRY *breaks
character.)*

HARRY: Nay! Stop! Thou hast taken this too far! We
coyly speak of sin and sin the more! Thy John and
Christ are sodomites!

KIT: Thou hast only now discovered this?

HARRY: Get out! I'll not burn on earth or in hell with
thee!

ACTOR: *(Appearing)* But I've not made my entrance yet!

HARRY: Thou'rt better off! Dost desire an entrance into
shame?

ACTOR: I read ahead. My best scene's coming up.

KIT: *(To* HARRY*)* Thou art out again until the end.
Prithee, let us finish the play, and if thou still despise it,
let me go.

HARRY: *(Pause, he looks to the* ACTOR.*)* If we quit the
play, thou hast won. Why plead to continue? What of
thy starving babes?

ACTOR: I want to play the scene.

HARRY: Very well. Declaim thy degradation.

(HARRY *sets himself apart from them and the* ACTOR *as*
JUDAS *launches into his next speech, a soliloquy.)*

ACTOR: *(As* JUDAS. *With a bag of silver)*
Now is the winter of our discontent
Made glorious summer by this carpenter.
But I, that am not shap'd for sportive tricks,
Nor made to court an amorous looking-glass;
Deform'd, unfinish'd, sent before my time
Into this breathing world, scarce half made up,
And that so lamely and unfashionable
That dogs bark at me as I halt by them—
Why, I, in this weak piping time of love,
Have no delight to pass away the time,
Unless to see my shadow in the sun
And descant on mine own deformity.
And therefore, since I cannot prove a lover
To entertain these fair well-spoken days,
I am determined to prove a villain
And hate the idle pleasures of these days.
Plots have I laid, inductions dangerous,
By drunken prophecies, potions, and dreams,
To make my lord's ambition more than mortal
And sow an avid hate among the priests.
He foolishly believes his public death
Will him Messiah prove when he doth rise.
But rise he shant, nor freely leave this green
Gethsemane—this bag of silver says.
Dive, thoughts, down to my soul, here Jesus comes!

KIT: *(As* JESUS. *Praying, as* JUDAS *hides)*
To be, or not to be, that is the question:
Whether 'tis nobler in the mind to suffer
The slings and arrows of outrageous fortune,
Or to take arms against a sea of troubles,
And by opposing, end them. To die, to sleep—
To sleep, perchance to dream—aye, there's the rub,
For in that sleep of death what dreams may come,

When we hve shuffled off this mortal coil,
Must give us pause; but soft you now, I see
Th' appointed Judas comes.

ACTOR: (*As* JUDAS. *Moved)*
The soldiers lurk
About us in the olive trees but no
Such branches do they peacefully bring thee.
Dost fear to die?

KIT: (*As* JESUS) Thou hast o'erheard my thoughts.

ACTOR: (*As* JUDAS) But thou shalt raise thee up.

KIT: (*As* JESUS) Thou knowst I can't.

ACTOR: (*As* JUDAS) Then wherefore wouldst thou die?

KIT: (*As* JESUS)
The martyr's words
Live longer in this world than tyrant laws.

ACTOR: (*As* JUDAS)
The priests and soldiers wait for me to sign
Thou art the man. The signal is a kiss.

KIT: (*As* JESUS)
Then kiss me now and show to me thy love.

ACTOR: (*As* JUDAS)
Thou art belov'd of John; let him kiss thee.
Or disappear into the close embrace
Of soft, dissembling night, escape, and live.
And I shall say that I am thee, and die.

KIT: (*As* JESUS) No greater love hath any man than this
To freely lay his life down for his friends.
Thou art belov'd of me as of this night.

(JESUS *kisses* JUDAS, *long and tenderly.* JUDAS *is
overwhelmed at first, but finally pushes* JESUS *away from
him and looks about himself in panic.)*

ACTOR: (*As* JUDAS. *Pointing at* JESUS *and shouting in Latin.*)
Ecce homo!

(HARRY *interrupts the scene.*)

HARRY: I understand! I understand thy play!
'Tis nothing but an atheist treatise, a palpitating blasphemy!

KIT: Thou thyself hast said a play may not be judged until the bows.

HARRY: When I—like a fond fool—defended thee to the Queen!

ACTOR: Amazed I am thou art not in the tower.

HARRY: (*Shudders, to* KIT) She said thy only course was suicide. Now I believe her.

KIT: (*Hurt for a moment*) Said she that?

ACTOR: You're to be arrested again tonight for atheism.

KIT: How knowst thou this?

ACTOR: You're not the only spy I know. Nicholas Skeres and Robert Poley spill their secrets for a crown or two. (*To* HARRY) Fly his cursed presence—thy money I spent may yet save thee. (*Quietly pockets the scattered pieces of silver.*)

KIT: (*Laughing*) The modern age breeds naught but Judases! (*Pointing to the* ACTOR) Thou, the Queen, Tommy, even that want-wit constable—have all betrayed me with concerted skill.

HARRY: Thou hast betrayed me with thy play. Good day, sirrah! (*Starts to leave*)

KIT: Hold! Dost only tonight grasp my meaning?

HARRY: It…only now grew irrefutable. 'Tis clearly devil's work.

KIT: And art surprised? From Faustus' creator? *(Begins to laugh)* Aye, I'd be the devil, if I believed in him!

ACTOR: Thou art!

HARRY: And sodomite as well!

KIT: Again—thou art amazed? *(Tears off his shirt, approaches* HARRY*)* Shall we wrestle like the Greeks?

HARRY: *(Moving away as* KIT *blocks his escape.)* I gave thee quarter—doubts—called thy sinful speeches courtly love.

KIT: Because you loved the sin.

HARRY: I never did!

KIT: Dost love it still. Thou art atremble—with desire?

HARRY: No! Let me go!

ACTOR: *(Tossing* HARRY *his knife)* Here, thy knife!

KIT: *(As* HARRY *catches the knife.)* 'Tis not the blade I seek.

HARRY: *(Brandishing the knife)* Thy sin shall kill thee—just as Her Majesty hath said—and thou wilt straight to hell.

KIT: *(Still advancing on* HARRY*)* There's neither hell nor heaven, I trow. But there is eternal life—through fame—give that to me.

HARRY: Not through this play.

ACTOR: Tear it into pieces—resurrect the goodly speeches in other plays. 'Tis only thy characters must die.

HARRY: *(Slashing at* KIT *with the knife)* Come not nearer.

KIT: *(Pressing his hand to the new cut in his side)* I changed my play for thee—was I deceived?

ACTOR: Let him touch thee not.

KIT: Thou lov'st me.

ACTOR: You can't!

KIT: *(To the* ACTOR*)* As once thou loved me.

ACTOR: Lies flow from thy mouth as from thy pen!

KIT: You've given me what you once had—innocence. For I trusted thee and proved myself a fool. And that, perhaps, is love.

*(*KIT *has gotten very close to* HARRY, *who has lowered the knife.)*

KIT: Wilt betray me with a kiss? *(Kisses* HARRY*)*

ACTOR: You'll burn!

(The ACTOR*'s shout jolts* HARRY *into action. He lifts the knife and brings it down between himself and* KIT, *as if to stab the kiss itself.)*

HARRY: No!

(The knife enters KIT*'s forehead just above the right eye.* KIT *staggers back, his forehead bleeding profusely from a deep wound. He clutches at the* ACTOR.*)*

KIT: Thou hast won, Willie.

ACTOR: It's William, damn you!

KIT: *(Falling against the wall, in a sitting position)* But e'en so, I scripted thee.

*(*KIT *dies in the sitting position, blood running down his face. His arm are extended in a semi-cruciform.* HARRY *and the* ACTOR *both stand there, trembling.)*

ACTOR: *(Cursing to hold back tears)* Bastard poet! Insisting on the last word.

HARRY: Kit! I'm sorry—please—! *(Crying, he starts toward* KIT.*)*

ACTOR: *(Stopping him. Taking the knife)* Robert Poley will be wanting this.

HARRY: Who? The spy? I'll be imprisoned, sure!

ACTOR: Nay.

HARRY: I've kilt a poet.

ACTOR: My lord, shut up. Thy crowns have bought us Skeres and Poley—they'll say they kilt him.

HARRY: You laid a plan for this?

ACTOR: Methought I did. But he had laid the plot and writ the scene. You were his suicide. His Judas.

(Placing the crown of thorns on KIT's head.)

HARRY: Thou art Judas.

ACTOR: Doth matter? He shall be remembered, not we.

HARRY: *(Desperately trying to wipe blood from his hand)* Then—shall I go? Oughtn't I? Come clean!

ACTOR: The play must perish as well.

HARRY: Yes! 'Tis implication of our intimacy— involvement— *(Collects the manuscript pages)* Let's burn them.

(The ACTOR lights a fire in a grate or fireplace; this may be done merely as an orange/red lighting effect. HARRY wipes the blood from his hands on the pages.)

HARRY: Will not thy false witnesses be tried for the deed?

ACTOR: The Queen wished him dead, did she not?

(HARRY nods.)

ACTOR: They'll be pardoned in a month. 'Tis arranged.

(HARRY starts to put the wad of paper in the fire.)

ACTOR: Not all at once. Singularly.

(HARRY hands the ACTOR a page. The ACTOR looks at it carefully, memorizing it, then lays it in the flames. HARRY continues handing him page after page and he continues memorizing them and burning them.)

HARRY: Are officers indeed on the way? Should we not make speed?

ACTOR: *(Memorizing)* I can go no faster.

HARRY: I like not the way he sits. 'Tis unnatural.

ACTOR: Touch him if you like. I must finish here.

(Gingerly at first, then tenderly, HARRY lays KIT out on the bed and wipes the blood from his face.)

HARRY: Come poet, take thy more comfortable rest. I meant not to kill thee. But you pressed me to it. With thy words, with thy wit, with thy glancing looks. *(Draping KIT in the JESUS costume)* I was thy John, and thou the blasphemous Christ. E'en now we save thy name by immolating thy lovely, profane play. Is that what you wanted? Is it? *(To the ACTOR)* Stop—can we—?

ACTOR: 'Tis gone. And we must go.

HARRY: We have sinned.

ACTOR: *(Gathering their possessions)* In executing a sinner?

HARRY: And his play.

ACTOR: 'Twas too rash, too true to live. As was he.

HARRY: But the beauteous speeches—now they are dead as well.

ACTOR: *(Escorting HARRY out the door, taps his own forehead)* Not a word. They all yet live. Farewell, rabbi. *(Looking almost wistfully at KIT as HARRY disappears.)*
Death, that hath suck'd the honey of thy breath,
Hath no power yet upon thy beauty:
Thou art not conquer'd, beauty's ensign yet
Is crimson in thy lips and in thy cheeks—

(The ACTOR *steps outside the door and closes it.* HARRY
immediately appears at another entrance as JOHN, *carrying
manuscript pages and the potion bottle.)*

HARRY: *(As* JOHN*)*
(Overlapping the ACTOR *and going to the dead* JESUS.*)*
Is crimson in thy lips and in thy cheeks—
And death's pale flag is not advanced there.
Why art thou yet so fair? Shall I believe
That unsubstantial Death is amorous,
And that the lean abhorred monster keeps
Thee here in dark to be his paramour?
For fear of that, I still will stay with thee,
And never from this palace of dim night
Depart again. O, thou art truly dead—
Not sleeping, soon to wake, but lifeless dust.
These three long days stretch to a month, a year—
No breath, no sign. Here, here will I remain
With worms that are thy chambermaids; O, here
Will I set up my everlasting rest,
And shake the yoke of inauspicious stars
From this world-wearied flesh. Eyes, look your last!
Arms, take your last embrace! and, lips, O you
The doors of breath, seal with a righteous kiss
A dateless bargain to engrossing death!
(Kisses JESUS.*)*
Come, bitter conduct, come, unsavory guide!
Thou desperate pilot, now at once run on
The dashing rocks thy sea-sick weary bark!
(Lifts the potion bottle to drink.)

KIT: *(As* JESUS. *Stirring)*
Sink not thy craft into the sea of woe.
The miracle, in faith, has come again.

HARRY: *(As* JOHN*)*
Thou liv'st! I saw thee hang and die—but liv'st!

KIT: *(As* JESUS) As I gazed in thy eyes from on the tree
When thou the hyssop raised with vinegar
To ease my parching thirst, I knew I'd live.

HARRY: *(As* JOHN)
'Twas not a vinegar-soaked sponge from which
Thou drank.
(Indicates potion bottle)
Some droplets from this bitter vial
I gave thee in the hope that it would prove
Thy life's salvation feigning chilly death.

(They stare at each other.)

HARRY: *(As* JOHN) 'Tis miracle no more?

KIT: *(As* JESUS) Our Lord cares not
How miracles are done, but that they are
Believ'd and lead believers to do good.
(Smiles, indicates the pages.)
Record the deed and thy words will resound.

(The ACTOR *appears in another part of the stage, sits down, and begins writing, much as* KIT *did earlier. He is dressed much better than before and seems prosperous, if not entirely happy. He also bears a remarkable resemblance to portraits of Shakespeare.)*

HARRY: *(As* JOHN)
I shall write and thou shalt live, but if
Thou wouldst, we must for Gaul depart apace.

KIT: *(As* JESUS) 'Tis not a noble act to flee, but I
Crave not a kingdom in this world, nor lord
It over men; the nobleness of life
Is to do thus—
(He embraces JOHN.*)*

HARRY: *(As* JOHN) And such a twain can do't.

ACTOR: *(Writing, with a sad smile)*
Dead shepherd, now I find thy saw of might:
Whoever lov'd that lov'd not at first sight?

KIT: *(As Jesus. Over* JOHN's *shoulder in the embrace.)*
Doubt not love's philosophy—
Lord, what fools these mortals be.

END OF PLAY

·

www.ingramcontent.com/pod-product-compliance
Lightning Source LLC
Chambersburg PA
CBHW052203090426
42741CB00010B/2384